Liqueured F....

For Karen and Glenn
'You can do anything if you set your mind to it.'

The Five Mile Press Pty Ltd
67 Rushdale Street
Knoxfield Victoria 3180 Australia

First published 1994

Text copyright © Joy Ross
Designer: Zoë Murphy
Photographer: Mannix
Food stylist: Tami McAdam
(assisted by Donna Normington)

All rights reserved. No part of this publication may be reproduced, stored in a retrieval system, or transmitted in any form or by any means, electronic, mechanical, photocopying, recording or otherwise, without the prior written permission of the Publishers.

Typeset by DigiType, Bendigo, Victoria
Printed in Singapore

National Library of Australia Cataloguing-in-Publication data

Ross, Joy.
Liqueured Fruit

Includes index
ISBN 0 86788 838 5

1. Cookery (Fruit). 2. Liqueurs. I. Title.

641.64

Acknowledgements

Special thanks to Glenda and Scott Bertram, Rosanna Traficante and John Travaglini. Extra special thanks to my artist husband Lance, who happily sketched for me.

Liqueured Fruit

Joy Ross

The Five Mile Press

Contents

Introduction	7
On a Practical Note	8
Cumquats	10
Tangelos	13
Apricots, Peaches, Plums and other Stone Fruits	14
Chestnuts	37
Quinces	41
Passionfruit	42
Grapes, Muscatels and Raisins	44
Grapefruit, Limes, Oranges and Lemons	57
Prunes and Figs	73
Pears	82
Pineapple	84
Berry Fruits	86
Leftover Fruit Liqueurs	93
Index	94

Introduction

I'm always surprised when visitors ask me to write down just how I liqueur fruit, because I find it so easy. You don't have to cook a thing! Liqueuring fruit is not new. In fact, some recipes come from my mother's recipe book, and these came in turn from her mother's. They are home-grown yet classic desserts that seem to have been largely forgotten.

Most liqueured fruits need at least two months to steep. But once this time is up you have a ready supply of liqueured fruit desserts just waiting to be eaten. And most fruit will be just as mouth-watering after twelve months. Some liqueured fruits, for example, pineapples in kirsch and cherry and orange fruit minces, may be used after just four weeks, while raisins in muscat are ready to use after only one or two weeks.

Many fruits lend themselves to being liqueured — for example, apricots, apples, cherries, cumquats, figs, grapefruit, grapes, lemons, nectarines, oranges, peaches, pineapples, plums, prunes, raspberries, strawberries, and many more. But always remember that if you're using fresh fruit the best time to liqueur it is when it's in season. When fruit is in abundance it is not only cheap (or free) but the size and flavour are at their best. It's important that you use only prime fruit for liqueuring. I find oranges, lemons and cumquats are the easiest to procure, because they are available throughout most of the year.

Be aware that when fruit is liqueured it becomes very rich in taste. So allow a maximum of three or four slices or chunks of fruit for each dinner guest. (On romantic occasions, individual pieces can be served as seductive finger-food!) Served with cream, ice-cream, custard, or in combination with suggested dishes, you will have a delicious gourmet dessert that doesn't make you tipsy. It's the old story, just as with chocolates — moderation in all things.

I've never found it hard to organise an entrée or main course for a dinner party, but sweets always used to be a time-consuming chore. But no longer — liqueur fruit desserts are so simple. And yet your guests are invariably impressed by their elegant sophistication.

So start today — and always have liqueured fruits in the pantry, ready to be used as 'instant' desserts. An added bonus is that you'll also end up with superb homemade fruit liqueurs. Good luck, and happy liqueuring!

JOY ROSS
Melbourne, 1994

On a Practical Note

BASIC METHOD

All you do is place your chosen fruit in a suitable sterilised jar or bottle. (Some fruits require pricking — this must always be done with a sterile needle.) To this you add the required amounts of sugar, alcohol and other ingredients, then clip your jar securely. Don't be afraid to experiment with different combinations of fruits and liqueurs — once you're used to the basic method you'll find it very easy, and a lot of fun.

It's important to remember that you should never fill the jars to the top. If you do, you tend to get a bit of spirit vacuum and the gasket doesn't seem to seal as well. So always leave a gap of 2–3 cm at the top of the jar.

You'll find that the sugar will drop to the base of the jar. So once a day, for about two weeks, either gently stir the sugar or turn your jars upside-down and back to the upright position. The sugar will gradually dissolve. For best results, store your fruit in a cool, dry place out of direct light.

Some cooks make up a sugar syrup to pour over their fruit. I find that messy and time-consuming and, besides, it takes the spontaneity out of liqueuring fruit — I much prefer the no-cook method.

STERILISING CONTAINERS

The easiest way of sterilising glass containers is to remove the rubber gaskets, then wash, dry and place jars in a 150°C oven for 15–20 minutes. Cool them before using and replace the freshly-washed rubber gaskets.

LABELLING JARS

As soon as you put your liqueured fruit into jars it is important to label and date it immediately. If you don't have time to make a creative label straight away just sticky-tape a note to the jar and improve the look of it when you are not so busy. An attractively-presented jar of liqueured fruit makes an excellent gift.

LIQUEURING DRIED FRUITS

When fresh fruit is not available you could try liqueuring dried fruit — either separately or in a dried fruit mix. Most dried fruits are sweeter than fresh, so I usually use half the amount of sugar. For example, for a 200-g packet of dried apricots I would use about 100 g of white sugar. You can experiment, adding more or less sugar depending on personal taste. Many varieties of nuts can also be liqueured.

A WORD ON ALCOHOL

You don't need to buy expensive spirits. The cheaper brands will work just as well. The flavour of brandy is possibly the most compatible with fruits, although many other spirits can be used — for example, Armagnac, gin, Grand Marnier, kirsch, rum, sherry, whisky, vodka, port, Madeira, Marsala, muscat, Tokay, grappa, Curacao, Cointreau, aquavit, and many others.

Fruit and sugar enhance the flavour of the alcohol, and you end up with not only liqueured fruit but homemade fruit liqueur as well. The latter may be used in a variety of ways. Obviously the easiest way is to drink it neat or reduce and strain the liqueur and serve it when you have friends in for liqueur and coffee. An Armagnac- or vodka-liqueured fruit base can even be served as an aperitif.

It's fun to experiment with fruit liqueurs. I often reduce the liquid in a saucepan over a low heat for about 15 minutes, then cool it and pour over ice-cream (see page 93). Liqueured brandy is stunning in a brandy sauce or custard. You can also add this superb fruity flavour to Christmas cakes and puddings. Even the humble ice-cream and jelly is enriched with fruit liqueur flavours.

~ Cumquats in Brandy ~

1 cup cumquats

1 cup sugar

enough brandy to cover fruit

1 medium sterilised clip-top jar

Wash and dry cumquats and prick all over with a sterile needle. Layer cumquats and sugar in jar, always remembering to leave a 2–3 cm gap at the top. Completely cover fruit with brandy. Clip jar securely.

The sugar will quickly fall to the base of the jar. Don't be concerned. During the next week or so, gently turn the jar upside-down and back to its upright position. Do this once a day. The sugar will eventually dissolve. Store for at least two to three months.

Cumquats are stunning served with amaretti biscuits and cream, see opposite and on page 12.

Opposite: *Amaretti Biscuits, Liqueured Cumquats and Cream, page 12*

Amaretti Biscuits with Liqueured Cumquats and Cream

250 g blanched almonds

2 egg-whites

1 cup caster sugar

300 ml cream, sweetened and whipped

1 medium jar drained liqueured cumquats

Put almonds in blender and process until finely ground.

Beat egg-whites until firm peaks form. Then fold in combined sugar and almonds. Roll heaped teaspoonfuls of mixture into balls and flatten with palms of hands.

Place on greased oven trays that have been lightly dusted with cornflour. Bake in moderately slow oven for about 20 minutes. Cool on tray.

My serving preference is to use a large plate and pile lots of drained cumquats in the centre. Whip the cream and place around cumquats. Circle the outer edge of the plate with amaretti biscuits.

This is a finger-food dessert. The idea is that guests take a biscuit, dip it into the cream and then take a piece of fruit. Truly delectable.

Tangelos in White Curacao

2 large tangelos

1 cup sugar

1 teaspoon Szechuan peppercorns

2 cloves

1 cinnamon stick

enough white Curacao to cover fruit

1 medium sterilised clip-top jar

I have always loved tangelos, but have only recently discovered that this fruit is a hybrid produced by crossing a tangerine tree with a grapefruit tree.

Wash and dry tangelos, but don't peel. Slice into 6-mm wedges, removing any hard membranes or pips. Place in jar and add peppercorns, cloves and cinnamon stick, leaving a small gap at the top. Pour sugar over and cover with Curacao.

Seal well and, for a couple of weeks, turn the jar upside-down and back once a day. This will help dissolve the sugar. Store for at least two months.

Liqueured tangelo slices are wonderful on their own, and the syrup makes a delicious sauce for ice-cream. Tangelo gelato is also great.

Liqueured Tangelo Gelato

1 medium jar liqueured tangelos

3 cups water

300 ml thickened cream

preserved ginger for garnish

Put liqueured tangelos (rinds and all) and liqueur, together with water, in a blender and process on high speed until mixture is smooth. Whip cream and fold into tangelo mixture. Pour into refrigerator trays and freeze. While freezing, stir mixture frequently with a fork. When gelato is set, flake with fork. Serve topped with strips of preserved ginger. Most refreshing!

Apricots in Grappa

1 kg firm apricots

2 cups sugar

enough grappa to cover fruit

¼ small lemon (grated rind only)

1 large or 2 small sterilised clip-top jars

Liqueured apricots taste wonderful, but they will lose some of their colour. I usually leave the stones in the apricots because they help to hold the shape of the fruit — but they can be pitted if you prefer. Wash and dry apricots. Prick each one with a sterile needle about six times.

Arrange apricots in layers in the jar, alternating them with sugar and lemon peel. Always leave a 2–3 cm gap at the top of the jar. Cover with grappa and clip jar securely.

The sugar will quickly fall to the base of the jar. Gently turn the jar upside-down and back, once a day, for the next couple of weeks. The sugar will eventually dissolve.

The apricots will be ready to eat in two to three months time.

Liqueured apricots are delicious on their own. And they are wonderful in a sago pudding, see opposite and on page 16.

Opposite: *Sago and Liqueured Apricot Pudding, page 16*

Sago and Liqueured Apricot Pudding

4 tablespoons sago

1 cup milk

1 cup drained liqueured apricots (reserve a few for garnish)

2 tablespoons liqueured grappa

1 cup soft breadcrumbs

1 cup sugar

1 teaspoon bicarbonate of soda

300 ml cream (optional)

Butterscotch Sauce

100 g butter

¼ cup brown sugar

2 tablespoons cream

¼ cup grappa liqueur

Soak the sago in the milk overnight.

Combine sago with remaining ingredients and spoon into a well-greased pudding basin or individual pudding moulds. Cover with lid or tied, buttered greaseproof paper.

Place the basin in a large saucepan with hot water coming three-quarters of the way up the pudding basin. Slowly cook over low heat for 2–3 hours depending on the size of the basin. Check water level from time to time.

Make butterscotch sauce by melting the butter in a saucepan, then adding in the other ingredients. Heat gently until boiling, then simmer for 3–4 minutes.

To serve: Upend the pudding onto a serving plate and top with a few extra apricots and the butterscotch liqueur sauce. Cut into slices and serve with or without cream. A nostalgic delight.

Apricots in Brandy

1 cup firm apricots

1 cup sugar

enough brandy to cover fruit

1 medium sterilised clip-top jar

Wash, dry and prick each apricot with a sterile needle about six times. Liqueured apricots tend to soften more than other fruit, so I don't remove the stones. They will lose their colour but not their flavour.

Loosely pack the jar with apricots and sprinkle sugar over, leaving a small gap at the top. Cover with brandy and clip the jar securely.

The sugar will quickly fall to the base of the jar. Don't be concerned. During the next week or so, gently turn the jar upside-down and back to its upright position. Do this once a day. The sugar will eventually dissolve.

The apricots will be ready to eat in about two months. Serve with clotted cream or incorporate them in the quick and easy recipe below.

Mascarpone with Liqueured Apricots

200 g fresh mascarpone cheese

¼ cup caster sugar

2–3 tablespoons apricot liqueur

5 chopped, drained, liqueured apricots

4 almond macaroons, finely crushed

Beat the mascarpone cheese with sugar and liqueur. Blend well. Fold through the chopped apricots and crushed macaroons.

Serve in individual glasses or cups. Decorate with whole apricots. Tempting and deliciously smooth.

Apricots in Marsala

1 kg firm apricots

2 cups sugar

enough Marsala to cover fruit

¼ lemon (grated rind only)

2 cloves

1 pinch ground cinnamon

1 medium sterilised clip-top jar

Wash and dry fruit. Prick each apricot with a sterile needle about six times. Stones can be removed but the apricots will retain their shape better if you leave them in.

Arrange the fruit in layers, alternating with layers of sugar, lemon rind, cinnamon and cloves, and leaving a small gap at the top of the jar. Cover fruit with Marsala and clip the jar securely.

The sugar will quickly fall to the base of the jar. Gently turn the jar upside-down and back, once a day for the next week or so. The sugar will eventually dissolve.

The apricots will be ready to serve in two to three months. The syrup from this fruit turns into a wonderful sauce or liqueur, while the apricots are heavenly on top of zabaglione.

Zabaglione and Marsala Apricots

8 large yolks

¼ cup sugar

½ cup Marsala fruit liqueur

½ cup dry white wine

300 ml thickened cream

½ teaspoon vanilla

drained liqueured apricots

In the top of a double boiler, off the heat, whisk the yolks together with the sugar until very foamy. Stir in the wine and Marsala. Put the pot over simmering water and stir continuously until the zabaglione begins to thicken. Don't boil or the eggs will curdle. Cool slightly. Pour into small bowls or glasses and refrigerate.

To serve: Whip the cream and vanilla. Top zabaglione and cream with drained liqueured apricots. Wonderful, or *meraviglioso* as the Italians would say.

Apricots in Vodka

1 cup firm apricots

¾ cup sugar

¼ lemon (grated rind only)

enough vodka to cover fruit

1 medium sterilised clip-top jar

Wash, dry and prick each apricot with a sterile needle about six times. Liqueured apricots tend to soften more than other fruits, so I don't remove the stones. They also lose their colour, but not their flavour.

Loosely pack jar with apricots and lemon rind, and sprinkle sugar over, leaving a small gap at the top. Cover with vodka and clip the jar securely.

The sugar will quickly fall to the base of the jar. During the next couple of weeks turn the jar upside-down, or use a spoon and gently move the sugar around in the jar. This will help the sugar to dissolve.

After about two months, pop a vodka-liqueured apricot in your mouth. Distinctively divine! Serve apricots on their own or on a cream cheese tart.

Vodka Apricot Custard Tart

500 g cream cheese

6 tablespoons sugar

2 tablespoons apricot vodka liqueur

3 tablespoons condensed milk

1 medium jar liqueured apricots

1 pastry case*

Cream cheese and add liqueur and sugar. Stir in condensed milk and mix well. Spread over pastry case.

Drain apricots and place on top of cheese mixture. Chill until served. I like to garnish each slice with a nasturtium flower. So simple and flavoursome!

*If you prefer to make your own pastry case, see the recipe for Glazed Blueberry Liqueur Tart (page 87).

~ *Dried Fruit in Madeira* ~

200 g dried apricots, pitted and whole

200 g dried pears

200 g dried or fresh cherries

1¼ cups white or brown granulated sugar

enough Madeira to cover fruit

2 medium sterilised clip-top jars

When fresh fruit is not available or is too expensive you can liqueur dried fruit. It provides a tasty and extremely easy alternative. Place layers of fruit and sugar in jars, leaving a small space at the top. (Brown sugar gives a darker and thicker liqueur, but don't fret if white sugar is all you have). Cover with Madeira and clip jar securely.

The sugar will quickly fall to the base of the jar. Don't be concerned. During the next week or so, gently turn the jar upside-down once a day. The sugar will eventually dissolve.

The fruit will be ready to eat after six weeks. A delicious snack with a cup of coffee and superb in Madeira fruit ice-cream.

Madeira Fruit Ice-cream

3 litres vanilla ice-cream

600 ml thickened cream

1 medium jar chopped liqueured apricots

1 empty 5-litre plastic ice-cream container with lid

Thaw ice-cream so that it can be stirred. Lightly sweeten and whip cream. In empty container mix one-third of the ice-cream, liqueured fruit and cream. Continue adding in this way until everything is mixed well. Refrigerate until firm.

To serve: Place some ice-cream in dessert glasses and decorate with a few pieces of liqueured fruit. A smart and refreshingly simple dessert.

Peaches in Brandy

1 kg peaches

2 cups sugar

2 cloves

1 cinnamon stick

enough brandy to cover peaches

1 large sterilised clip-top jar

Like apricots, peaches get a bit ragged if they are halved. Wash, dry and prick each whole peach with a sterile needle, about nine times. Pack into jar with cloves, add cinnamon stick and sugar, but don't fill the jar to the top. Cover with brandy and clip jar carefully. Steep for two to three months.

Once a day, over the next few weeks, hold the jar on both the top and base and gently move the sugar around. It will eventually dissolve.

Peaches in brandy are superb with cold custard. If you want a scrumptious, warm dessert try them topped with meringue.

Warmed Liqueured Peaches with Meringue

5 egg-whites

60 g caster sugar

3 yolks

20 g flour

10 g unsalted butter

25 ml milk

1 large jar liqueured peaches

cream for garnish (optional)

Preheat oven to 220°C. Butter a large but not too deep pie-dish and place a semi-drained layer of peaches on the base. Beat egg-whites until stiff. Continue beating and gradually add caster sugar until the meringue has peaks.

Beat yolks with fork and add a little bit of egg-white to obtain a thicker texture. Fold into main egg-whites, add flour and carefully mix through.

Melt butter and add milk. Pour over peaches. Now spread egg-white mixture over peaches.

Cook in hot oven for about 6–8 minutes or until the meringue is lightly golden and puffy. Serve immediately. We usually pour a little unsweetened cream over the top of each serve. Peaches and cream at its best!

Peaches in Grand Marnier

500 g peaches

1 cup brown sugar

1 small orange (grated rind only)

enough Grand Marnier to cover peaches

2 medium sterilised clip-top jars

Wash, dry and prick each whole peach with a sterile needle, about nine times. Layer in jars with brown sugar and orange rind, leaving a small gap at the top. Cover with Grand Marnier and clip jar securely. Store for at least two months.

Once a day over the next few weeks, gently stir sugar in jars. This helps it to dissolve.

Peaches in Grand Marnier are mouthwatering when simply placed on individual plates, topped with whipped cream and drizzled in their own liqueur. And peach-liqueured Grand Marnier is wonderful with snow eggs.

Snow Eggs with Liqueured Peach Sauce

3 egg-whites

100 g sugar

300 ml milk

½ vanilla pod

1 medium jar Grand Marnier peach liqueur

Before making the snow eggs, place the peach liqueur in a saucepan and simmer on a low heat to thicken slightly. Allow about 8–10 minutes.

To make the snow eggs, whip the egg-whites until very stiff. Keep whipping and gradually add sugar.

Cut the vanilla pod lengthwise and place in a shallow saucepan with the milk. Bring to the boil, then reduce to just under boiling point. At this stage, check the reducing liqueur on stove. It's probably ready to turn off. Coat a tablespoon with the heated milk and use it to shape 'eggs' from the egg-white mixture. Poach 'eggs' in hot milk for about 3 minutes on either side.

Pour reduced liqueur into two slightly curved plates, and top with equal portions of snow eggs. Soft and exquisite.

Peaches in Marsala

1 kg peaches
2 cups brown sugar
1 lemon
enough Marsala to cover peaches
1 large sterilised Mason jar*

Wash and dry peaches. Squeeze lemon. Prick peaches about nine times with a sterile needle, and wipe with lemon juice. Place peaches in jar, cover with sugar and pour Marsala over, leaving a 2–3 cm gap at the top. I usually place a piece of plastic wrap between jar and screw-top lid.

Once a day, over the next few weeks, hold the jar on both the top and base and gently move the sugar around. It will eventually dissolve.

You could serve the peaches whole, or halved and stoned. Pour a little liqueur over them and decorate with a sprig of mint. A frozen nut cream is an appealing alternative.

* These screw-top jars are available at most hardware shops and department stores.

Liqueured Peaches in Frozen Nut Cream

250 g liqueured peaches, drained and mashed
100 g Neufchatel cheese
½ cup caster sugar
½ cup evaporated milk, well-chilled
1 tablespoon hazelnuts, chopped
2 egg-whites
Marsala liqueur for drizzling

Beat Neufchatel until smooth and add the sugar. Mix well. Add chilled, evaporated milk and beat until a little thicker and creamier. Fold in mashed liqueured peaches and hazelnuts (or other nuts if you prefer). Whip egg-whites until stiff. Thoroughly but gently fold into cream mixture. Pour into empty ice-cream container, cover and freeze until firm. Remove and beat a second time to make the dessert creamier. Cover and return to freezer.

When ready to serve, place scoops on plates and drizzle with your favourite homemade liqueur. Sweet, seductive and filling.

Plums in Aquavit

1 kg plums, ripe and not too large
3 cups brown sugar
1 pod vanilla
1 lemon (grated rind only)
4 teaspoons peppermint tea
2 cups water
enough aquavit to cover plums
1 large sterilised Mason jar

Aquavit is a potato-based spirit which complements the flavour of the plums. Unlike most fruit, you can eat these plums after only three weeks. There's no need to pit them.

Place peppermint tea in large bowl, and pour about two cups of boiling water over it. When the tea is brewed and lukewarm, add the washed, dried and pricked plums (prick each plum about six times with a sterile needle) and steep for at least one hour. If you do this in the evening let them steep until morning.

Place drained plums in jar, leaving a small space at the top. Add vanilla pod, lemon rind and pour sugar over the fruit. Cover with aquavit, and seal the jar tightly. I usually place a piece of plastic wrap between the jar and the screw-top lid. Over the next few weeks, stir the sugar once a day. This will help dissolve the sugar.

For a really refreshing dessert try this liqueured plum sorbet.

Liqueured Plum Sorbet

1 medium jar drained liqueured plums
1 egg-white
½ cup aquavit plum liqueur
extra liqueured plums or fresh fruit

Remove stones from the plums, which will now be beautifully soft. Place all the plums and ½ cup of plum liqueur in food processor and blend until smooth. Pour mixture into shallow pan, cover and freeze until firm.

Remove frozen plum mixture from freezer, process again and add egg-white. Cover and refreeze until ready to use. Scoop onto individual plates and drizzle a little aquavit plum liqueur over. Decorate with extra liqueured plums or fresh fruit. Iced liqueured fruit at its best.

Plums in Brandy

1 kg plums, firm blood plums preferred

3½ cups sugar

enough brandy to cover fruit

1 large sterilised Mason jar

Remember this recipe in summer, when lots of people have plum-laden trees and don't know what to do with all the fruit. Add one kilogram of sugar instead of 3½ cups if you want a sweeter result — so you have roughly equal quantities of plums, sugar and brandy.

Wash and drain plums and prick each one about six times with a sterile needle. Place in the large jar (stopping short of the top) and pour sugar and brandy over. Screw lid on carefully and keep six weeks. Liqueured plums can be stored for at least a year, although they may lose a bit of their sweetness.

Once a day, over the next few weeks, hold the top and bottom of the jar and gently move sugar. It will eventually dissolve.

Liqueured plums and cream are an old family favourite. For a more elaborate dessert, try this liqueured marshmallow cake.

Liqueured Marshmallow Cake

3 egg-whites

3 heaped teaspoons gelatine

1 cup water

1 cup sugar

3 level teaspoons granulated coffee

1 medium jar drained liqueured plums

300 ml whipped cream (optional)

Beat eggs, and slowly add sugar (into which coffee has been mixed) until fluffy. On stove, melt gelatine in half a cup of water. Pour back in cup and add half cup of cold water. Add slowly, one dessertspoon at a time, to the egg-white mixture. Continue beating for 5 minutes.

Pour mixture into a shallow pie dish lined with 25 cm greaseproof paper (shiny side up). Refrigerate at least one hour.

To serve: Upend cake, peel away greaseproof paper and place on serving plate. Decorate with drained plums and pour some of the liqueured plum brandy over the entire cake. Place bowl of whipped cream on table, for those who want it. Impressive and different.

Nectarines in Brandy

450 g nectarines

1½ cups brown sugar

enough brandy to cover nectarines

2 medium sterilised clip-top jars

Wash, halve and stone the nectarines. Place equal amounts of fruit in jars, leaving a slight gap at the top. Pour sugar over and cover with brandy.

Once a day over the next couple of weeks, turn jars upside-down and back again. This will dissolve the sugar. Store for about four weeks. Serve as a delectable nibble or stuffed in creamed profiteroles.

Profiteroles Filled with Brandied Nectarines

75 g butter, chopped

1 cup water

1 cup flour

4 eggs

300 ml thickened cream

1 medium jar of liqueured nectarines for garnish

Preheat oven to 220°C. Combine butter and water in saucepan and bring to the boil. When butter has melted and water is boiling add sifted flour. Stir vigorously until mixture leaves side of saucepan and forms a smooth ball. Transfer mixture to a bowl and add eggs one at a time, beating well after each addition. You will end up with a glossy mixture.

Place teaspoonfuls of mixture, about 5 cm apart, on a greased oven tray. Bake in hot oven for 10 minutes, reduce heat to moderate and cook a further 15 minutes or until puffs are lightly brown and crisp. Take out of oven and quickly make a small slit in the side of the puffs. This allows steam to escape. Return to moderate oven for about 10 minutes or until dry.

Cool and then cut in half. Remove soft mixture from centre and fill with whipped cream and a liqueured nectarine. Dust with icing sugar. A taste and texture delight!

Nectarines in Peach Brandy

900 g nectarines

3 cups sugar

enough peach brandy to cover nectarines

1 large sterilised Mason jar

Halve and stone the nectarines and place in Mason jar. Cover them with sugar, then pour peach brandy over them. Leave a space at top of jar, screw securely and store for about two months. I usually place a piece of plastic wrap between the jar and metal or plastic lid.

Once a day, for a couple of weeks, hold the jar securely on both the top and base and gently move the sugar around. It will eventually dissolve.

Liqueured nectarines make an impressive mousse.

Nectarine Brandy Mousse

8 drained liqueured nectarine halves

¾ cup fresh raspberries

3 tablespoons peach brandy liqueur

1 tablespoon gelatine

3 tablespoons fresh lemon juice

½ cup granulated sugar

¼ teaspoon almond essence

pinch of salt

½ cup thickened cream

2 egg-whites

Purée liqueured nectarines, raspberries and peach brandy liqueur.

In a saucepan, soak gelatine in lemon juice for 5 minutes. Add puréed fruit, sugar, almond essence and salt. Stir continuously and bring to boil. Remove from heat, transfer to a bowl and cool.

Whip cream to soft peaks and gently fold into fruit mixture. Refrigerate until mixture begins to set (about one hour).

Beat egg-whites until stiff. Gently fold half the egg-whites into mousse. Fold in remaining egg-whites, making sure there are no lumps.

Spoon into glasses or a serving bowl. Chill for 4 hours before serving. Place one or two lightly drained liqueured nectarines on top of each serve. Wonderfully smooth and luscious.

~ *Cherries in Brandy* ~

500 g fresh cherries

1 cup sugar

1 small orange (grated rind only)

enough brandy to cover fruit

1 large or 2 medium sterilised clip-top jars

Remove the cherry stones if you wish — but I don't. Wash and drain the cherries and prick each one about six times with a sterile needle. Place them and orange rind in sterilised jar, stopping 2–3 cm short of the top.

Pour sugar over mixture and cover with brandy. Clip the jar securely. The sugar will quickly fall to the base of the jar. Don't be concerned. Once a day, during the next couple of weeks, gently turn the jar upside-down. Return to upright position. The sugar will eventually dissolve.

Leave for at least six weeks. If properly stored on a cool, dry shelf the cherries will keep for at least a year. Serve with coffee or cherry liqueur money biscuits.

Cherry Liqueur Money Biscuits

250 g plain sweet biscuits

100 g Neufchatel cheese

1 tablespoon caster sugar

1 large egg

1 tablespoon cherry brandy liqueur

1½ tablespoons chopped liqueured cherries

silver or gold foil (optional)

Crush biscuits in food processor or with rolling pin.

Beat the Neufchatel cheese until smooth and add sugar and egg. Beat well.

Add the biscuit crumbs, cherry liqueur and chopped cherries and mix well. Refrigerate for 15 minutes.

Form the mixture in a roll, about 5 cm in diameter, on aluminium foil or plastic wrap. Refrigerate overnight.

To serve, cut the roll into 1-cm slices and carefully wrap in silver or gold foil. Exquisitely rich and a bit of fun.

Cherries in Grand Marnier

1 kg cherries

1 cup sugar

1 cinnamon stick

enough Grand Marnier to cover fruit

1 large sterilised clip-top jar

Wash and dry cherries, then prick each one about six times with a sterile needle. Layer fruit and sugar in jar, placing the cinnamon stick at the halfway mark. Don't fill the jar to the top. Cover with Grand Marnier and clip the jar securely.

Occasionally turn the jar upside-down and back again to dislodge the sugar on base of jar. It will eventually dissolve. Leave for two to three months before serving.

You can do virtually anything with liqueured cherries. Enjoy them separately or with other fruit and cream. Served with Bombe Alaska, they add a potent bite.

Liqueured Cherry Bombe Alaska

oblong sponge or plain cake (bought)

2-litre brick vanilla ice-cream

4 egg-whites

¼ teaspoon salt

8 tablespoons sugar

1 medium jar liqueured cherries

Pre-heat oven to 230°C. Slightly soften ice-cream.

Trim cake so that it's 25 mm wider on all sides than the brick of ice-cream. Beat egg-whites until foamy, add salt and continue beating until stiff. Gradually add sugar.

Place ice-cream on cake. Spread meringue over cake and ice-cream, making sure that the meringue completely covers the ice-cream.

Bake *bombe* on a baking sheet for 5 minutes or until the meringue is lightly browned. Cut into slices, drizzle with cherry liqueur and place liqueured cherries alongside. Rather scrumptious.

 Cherries in Grappa

1 cup cherries

1 cup brown or white granulated sugar

enough grappa to cover fruit

1 medium sterilised clip-top jar

I've kept this liqueur fruit recipe fairly basic because I'm adding the cherries to a nut ice-cream, and so extra flavour is not necessary.

I always wash my fruit in a colander. Drain and prick each cherry about six times with a sterile needle. Then place in jar and pour sugar over. Cover with grappa, leaving a 2–3 cm gap at the top of the jar, and clip securely.

Occasionally turn the jar upside-down to dislodge the sugar on the base of jar. Return to upright position. The sugar will eventually dissolve.

The cherries can be left for up to a year, but after six weeks they will be ready to eat or to add to the ice-cream recipe.

Liqueured Cherry Ice-cream

300 ml thickened cream

1 tablespoon caster sugar

1 egg, separated

1 tablespoon chopped hazelnuts

1 cup drained, roughly-chopped liqueured cherries*

1 teaspoon cherry grappa liqueur

Beat the egg-white until it forms stiff peaks. Beat the cream and sugar together until thick and fold the two together. Beat the yolk and carefully fold into the mixture. Add the cherries, liqueur and nuts.

Rinse out a jelly mould or basin with water and pour the mixture into it. Cover with foil and freeze for about 3 hours. Slightly warm base of container. Upend ice-cream onto serving plate. Serve in thin slices and decorate with whole cherries.

This makes a great cold Christmas pudding. Sweet ecstasy!

* Reserve some cherries to decorate ice-cream slices.

Cherries in Kirsch

1 kg cherries

1 cup sugar

1 cinnamon stick

2 star anise (optional)

enough kirsch to cover fruit

1 large sterilised clip-top jar

Wash and dry cherries, then prick each one about six times with a sterile needle. Layer fruit and sugar in jar, placing cinnamon stick and star anise at the halfway mark. Cover with kirsch, leaving a small gap at the top of the jar, and clip securely.

Occasionally turn the jar upside-down, or move cherries with a spoon and dislodge the sugar on the base of the jar. The sugar will eventually dissolve. Leave for two to three months before serving.

Kirsch Soufflé

300 ml milk

100 g sugar

1 teaspoon vanilla essence

75 g butter

50 g flour

5 yolks, beaten

75 ml cherry kirsch liqueur

6 egg-whites, beaten to soft peaks

1 medium jar drained liqueured cherries

Bring milk, sugar and vanilla to boiling point.

Melt the butter in a large heavy-bottomed saucepan. Sift in the flour little by little, stirring well. When the mixture is bubbling, add the boiling milk in a steady stream. Bring back to the boil and beat all the time until thick and smooth. Remove from the heat and allow to cool a little. Beat in the yolks and your homemade liqueur.

Liberally butter four large soufflé dishes and dust with sugar. Carefully incorporate the egg-whites into the soufflé mixture and pour into the mould. Cook at 190°C for 20–25 minutes. Place individual soufflé dishes on white plates and circle with liqueured cherries. Rich and most rewarding.

Morello Cherries in Rum

2 kg morello cherries

2 cups sugar

1 vanilla pod

1 cinnamon stick

enough white rum to cover fruit

1 large sterilised clip-top jar

These dark red cherries make a richly-coloured liqueur and they swell beautifully. Wash cherries and prick each one about six times with a sterile needle. Put half the cherries in the jar, place cinnamon stick and vanilla pod vertically and add remaining fruit. Pour sugar and then white rum over cherries, leaving a 2–3 cm gap at the top of the jar. Clip securely.

Occasionally turn the jar upside-down to dislodge the sugar on the base of jar. Return to upright position. The sugar will eventually dissolve.

Keep for at least two months. It will be well worth the wait. I love chocolate and cherry combinations, so I sometimes make an almond chocolate cake and drizzle cherry liqueur over the wedges.

Choc-a-holics' Cherry Chocolate Cake

125 g butter

¾ cup caster sugar

6 eggs, separated

125 g dark chocolate, grated

2 cups ground almonds

⅓ cup dry white breadcrumbs

1 tablespoon cherry rum liqueur

extra cherry liqueur for garnish

Line and grease a 23-cm round cake tin. Cream butter and sugar in small bowl until light and fluffy, add yolks and beat well. Transfer mixture to large bowl, stir in chocolate, almonds, breadcrumbs and rum liqueur.

Beat egg-whites until soft peaks form, then fold through almond mixture in two lots. Pour into prepared cake tin and bake in moderate oven about 40–50 minutes.

Stand for 5 minutes before turning cake onto rack. Cool. Serve in wedges and drizzle with your cherry liqueur. Garnish alongside with liqueured morello cherries. A choc-a-holic's fantasy!

Cherries in Vodka

1 cup cherries

1 cup sugar

enough vodka to cover fruit

1 medium sterilised clip-top jar

To use these cherries in the cherry cake recipe below you must remove the stones. If you do this while you are watching television it doesn't seem to take any time at all!

Gently wash and lightly dry cherries. Prick at random with a sterile needle, and then place in jar. Pour sugar over and cover both with vodka, leaving a 2–3 cm gap at the top of the jar. Clip securely.

Don't shake or invert these pitted cherries. They are too delicate. With a spoon, gently dislodge the sugar on the base of jar every day. It will eventually dissolve.

Leave for at least six weeks before nibbling or including in this wonderful cherry cake.

Liqueured Cherry Cake

3 eggs, beaten

4 tablespoons caster sugar, plus extra for dusting

125 g plain flour, sifted

1 teaspoon dried yeast

milk

1 medium jar of liqueured cherries, drained, stones removed

Beat the eggs and sugar together. Slowly add the flour, then the yeast. Mix well. Add enough milk to make a smooth and not-too-thin pancake batter. Butter a flan dish and pour in the batter. Arrange the cherries on top.

Bake in a hot oven, 222°C, for 30–35 minutes. The cake will be done when it is golden-brown and when a skewer pushed into the middle comes out clean.

Dust with caster sugar and serve warm or cold. Captivatingly tasty.

Cherry Fruit Mince in Rum

350 g glacé cherries

250 g cooking apples, peeled, cored and grated

175 g raisins

125 g currants

125 g sultanas

100 g walnuts, chopped

100 g butter

375 g brown sugar

5 ml mixed spice

400 ml rum, dark

enough medium sterilised clip-top jars or one large Mason jar

Place all the ingredients in a large bowl. Mix well together, cover and leave for two days. Stir well and pour into jars. Secure tightly and stand at least two weeks.

I make this colourful liqueured fruit mince around Christmas. It's great to put in mince pies.

An even easier way to serve it is to make a circle of fruit mince on individual medium-sized serving plates and pour brandy sauce into the centre, see opposite and on page 35.

Opposite: *Cherry Mince with Christmas Brandy Sauce, page 36*

Cherry Mince with Christmas Brandy Sauce

Brandy Sauce

12 eggs

250 g unsalted butter, cut into pieces

400 g sugar

200 ml orange juice

100 ml brandy*

1 tablespoon fruit mince per person

300 ml whipped cream (optional)

Place all ingredients, except brandy, into a double saucepan over a high heat. Whisk until thick. This takes about 3-4 minutes.

Place top saucepan in cold water and continue whisking until sauce is cold. Whisk in brandy. Serve the cherry mince and brandy chilled or heat both fruit and sauce if you want a warm dessert. You'll be tempted to have seconds, whether you add the cream or not.

*If you have any brandy liqueur left over from any other liqueured fruit, use that instead of orange juice and brandy. It makes a top sauce.

Chestnuts in Grappa

1 kg fresh chestnuts

1½ cups sugar

enough grappa to cover fruit

2 medium sterilised clip-top jars

Some Italian friends told me how to liqueur chestnuts in grappa — that wonderful spirit distilled from the fermented remains of grapes after pressing. Simply boil the chestnuts in their shells, in plenty of water. The shells will soon begin to open. Once this happens, take off stove and drain. As soon as they can be handled, remove as much of the thin outer shell as possible without breaking them.

Divide nuts and sugar between the two jars and cover both with grappa. Clip the jars securely. Always finish 2–3 cm short of the top of the jars.

During the next week or so, tip the jars to the side and back again. The sugar will eventually dissolve. Keep in a cool, dark place for two to three months.

A liqueured chestnut served with coffee really completes a meal. As an alternative, chestnuts with *crème anglaise* make a simple and punchy dessert. When nuts are liqueured they are very filling, so two or three chestnuts per serve is plenty.

Liqueured Chestnuts with Crème Anglaise

500 ml milk

3 teaspoons sugar

6 yolks

1 teaspoon vanilla essence

1 medium jar drained liqueured chestnuts

fresh fruit for garnish

Bring milk to the boil. Beat sugar and yolks until pale and thick. Pour in milk and return mixture to the saucepan.

Cook over low heat, stirring all the time until crème/custard coats the back of the spoon. Strain into a bowl and add vanilla. Cool and refrigerate. Serve liqueured chestnuts on a bed of *crème anglaise*. Garnish with fresh fruit. Pleasurably creamy and crunchy.

Chestnuts in Grand Marnier

1 kg chestnuts (or hazelnuts or pistachios)

1½ cups sugar

1 small orange (grated rind only)

enough Grand Marnier to cover chestnuts

2 medium sterilised clip-top jars

Crunchy liqueured nuts are a fun alternative to liqueured fruit. They take more time than fruit, but are certainly worth the effort. If you don't have Grand Marnier you can use kirsch or white rum.

Boil the chestnuts in their shells, in plenty of water. It doesn't take long before the shells begin to open. Once this happens, take off stove and drain. As soon as the chestnuts can be handled remove as much of the thin outer shell as possible without breaking them.

Layer nuts, sugar and orange rind in jars. Always finish layering 2–3cm short of the top of the jar. Cover chestnuts with Grand Marnier and clip jars securely.

The sugar will quickly fall to the base of the jars. Don't be concerned. During the next week or so, tip the jars to the side and back again. The sugar will eventually dissolve. Keep in a cool, dark place for at least two to three months.

Chestnuts are delicious when served with whipped cream. I like to go a bit further and decorate a strawberry meringue torte, see opposite and on page 40.

Opposite: *Liqueured Chestnuts on Strawberry Meringue Torte, page 40*

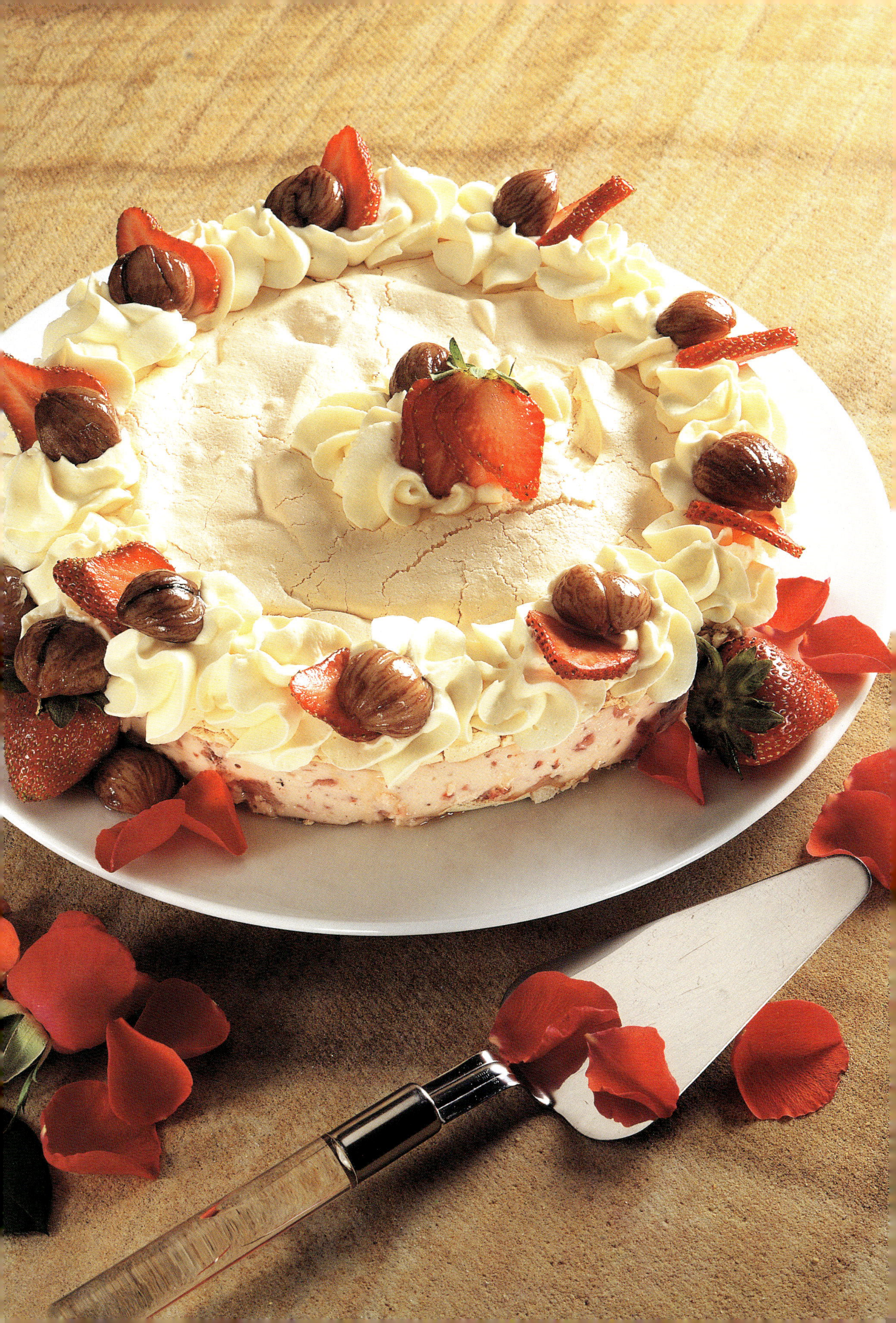

Liqueured Chestnuts on Strawberry Meringue Torte

Meringue

3 egg-whites

1 cup sugar

1 cup slivered almonds

¼ cup plain flour

Beat egg-whites until peaks form. Gradually add sugar, and beat until dissolved. Combine almonds and flour and fold in meringue. Spread half the mixture evenly over the base of a greased and floured 25-cm springform tin.

Bake in moderately slow oven for 25 minutes. Cool for 5 minutes and remove from base with knife. Cool on wire rack. Repeat with remaining mixture.

Strawberry Mousse

2 punnets strawberries

3 yolks

½ cup caster sugar

1 tablespoon gelatine

¼ cup water

600 ml bottle thickened cream, whipped

1 medium jar liqueured chestnuts

Wash strawberries and remove husks. Purée strawberries until smooth. Pour into large bowl. Beat yolks and sugar in small bowl until thick and pale and fold into strawberry mix.

Sprinkle gelatine over water, heat to gently dissolve. Cool to room temperature and add to strawberry mixture. Fold in whipped cream.

To assemble: Cover one base and sides of springform tin with tinfoil. Place first meringue on base and pour mousse. Refrigerate until set. Cover with remaining meringue and dust with icing sugar.

Leave in refrigerator for at least half a day so that meringue softens slightly. This makes cutting easier.

Decorate with drained liqueured chestnuts. Serve each guest with a wedge of meringue and a glass of chestnut-liqueured Grand Marnier. Fabulous or *favoloso* as the Italians might say.

Quinces in Vodka

500 g quinces

2 cups sugar

1 lemon (grated rind only)

3 pods cardamom

1 teaspoon Szechuan peppercorns (optional)

enough vodka (or gin) to cover quinces

1 large sterilised clip-top jar

Wash, peel, core and cut quinces into thick chunks or slices. Layer in jar with sugar, lemon, cardamom pods and peppercorns, leaving a small gap at the top. Cover in vodka and seal well.

Dissolve the sugar over the next couple of weeks by daily tipping the jar upside-down and back again. Store for about three months.

Quinces are wonderful simply served in their liqueur juice.

Quinces in Jelly Russe with Sponge Fingers

1 packet sponge fingers

1 packet red jelly

300 ml thickened cream

3 tablespoons milk

1 dessertspoon gelatine

½ cup warm water

25 g sugar

vanilla essence

1 medium jar drained liqueured quinces

extra cream for garnish, if desired

Make the jelly and pour half into a 16-cm cake tin or mould. Cut the sponge fingers to the height of tin and line sides. Place in coldest part of the refrigerator for 10 minutes. Remove and gently press drained liqueured quinces on top.

Pour rest of jelly over and return to refrigerator. Soak gelatine in water, and dissolve without boiling. Warm milk and sugar and, beating quickly with a fork, slowly add tepid gelatine. Semi-whip cream and add milk mixture. Cool and add vanilla essence. Stir occasionally until it starts to set. Pour into prepared mould. Refrigerate to set.

To serve: Slightly warm base of tin. Invert. If desired, garnish with extra cream or liqueur. Fun to make — and to eat.

Passionfruit in White Rum

2 cups passionfruit pulp, fresh
1 cup brown sugar
enough white rum to cover passionfruit
1 medium sterilised clip-top jar

It's hard to estimate how many passionfruit you'll need to obtain two cups of pulp because some fruits have more flesh than others. I used about twelve, but remember that only moist pulp should be used. This is an easy recipe, so just vary the other quantities according to the amount of passionfruit pulp.

Simply pulp the passionfruit, add to the jar and pour the sugar and white rum over. Leave a 2–3 cm gap at the top of the jar. Clip securely and store at least two months. For the next couple of weeks, however, hold the jar on both top and base once a day and gently move the sugar around. This will help dissolve it.

Passionfruit is a semi-liquid fruit, but makes a thick liqueur. When I need to make a dessert in a hurry there's nothing easier than adding whipped cream to softened vanilla ice-cream and folding through some liqueured passionfruit. This makes a quick and sensuous St Valentine's Day sweet. On the other hand, if you have the time and want to show a bit more expertise, try the St Valentine's Day passion soufflé, see opposite and on page 44.

Opposite: *St Valentine's Day Passion Soufflé, page 44*

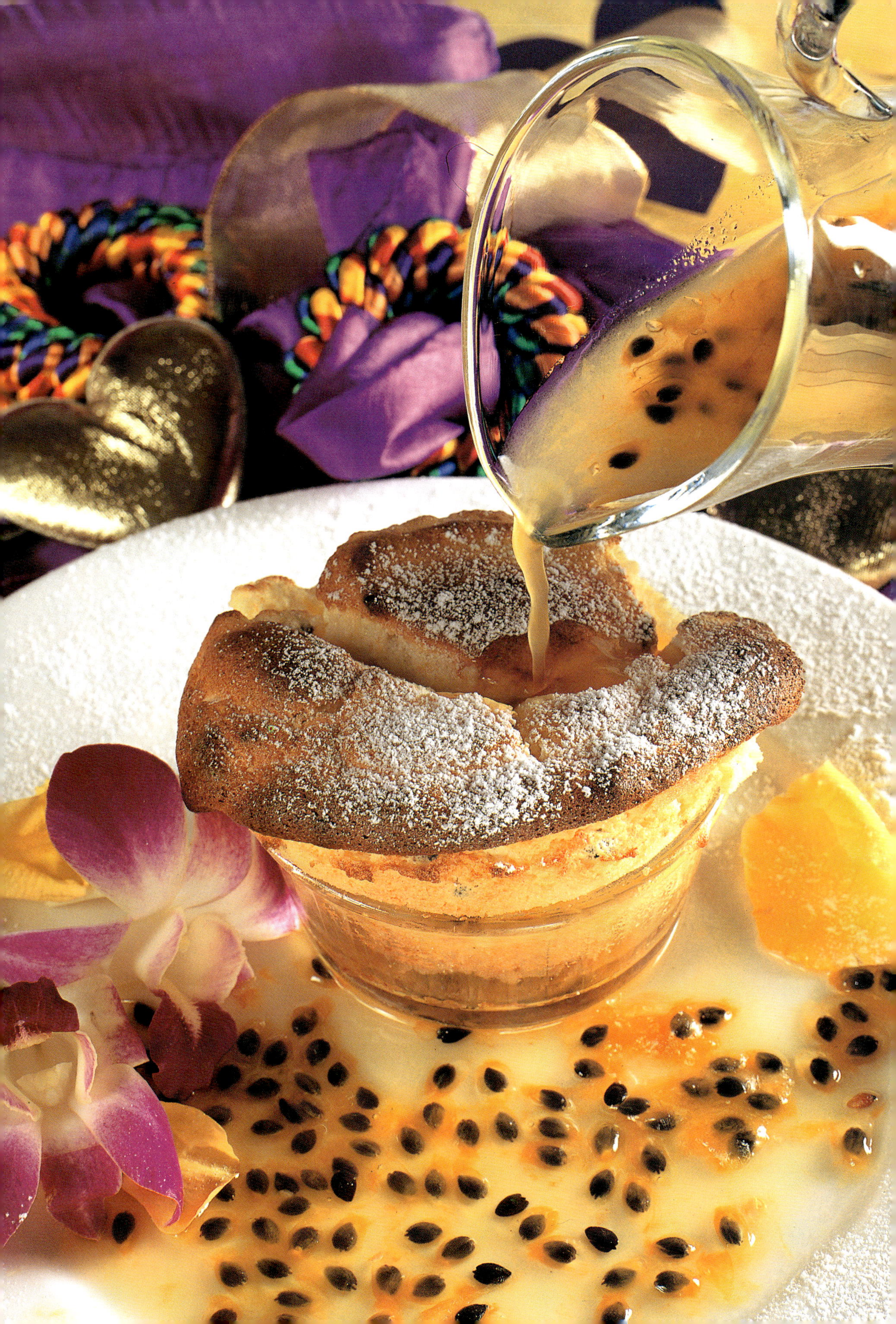

St Valentine's Day Passion Soufflé

4 yolks

200 g caster sugar

8 egg-whites

500 g drained liqueured passionfruit pulp

icing sugar

This is a wonderfully romantic St Valentine's Day dessert. Butter and sprinkle with sugar four large soufflé moulds. Preheat oven to 220°C.

Beat the egg yolks with half the sugar until light and fluffy. In another bowl, beat whites, adding the remaining sugar in small amounts. Continue beating until whites stand as shiny, firm peaks.

Add three tablespoons of passionfruit pulp to the yolks, mix well and stir in a quarter of the egg-whites. Thoroughly but gently fold in rest of egg-whites. Pour soufflé mixture into moulds and cook in hot oven for about 10 minutes or until soufflés puff up and brown lightly.

While the soufflé is cooking warm some extra liqueured passionfruit pulp. The soufflé is much better if served hot.

Dust with icing sugar and drizzle with warmed liqueured pulp. A special way of saying 'I love you'.

Grapes in Armagnac

500 g large firm grapes (not sultana)

1 cup white sugar

1 tablespoon coriander seeds

1 small orange (grated peel only)

enough Armagnac to cover grapes

1 large sterilised clip-top jar

Wash and dry grapes and leave them on small stems. Place them in jar with orange peel and coriander. Pour sugar over, cover with Armagnac, and leave 2–3 cm gap at top of jar. Secure jar and keep for at least three weeks. To dissolve the sugar, turn jar upside-down and back daily, or gently stir sugar with a long-handled spoon. I sometimes serve a bunch of liqueured grapes alongside a piece of walnut tart, see opposite.

Armagnac Grapes and Walnut Tart

Pastry

250 g flour, sifted

100 g butter, softened

50 g caster sugar

2 yolks

pinch of salt

Filling

125 g walnuts, chopped

300 ml thickened cream

½ teaspoon vanilla essence

100 g caster sugar

1 egg-white, beaten until stiff

pinch of salt

Icing

50 ml liqueured grape Armagnac

100 g icing sugar

10 walnut halves

1 medium jar liqueured grapes for garnish

Mix pastry ingredients together to form a ball. Refrigerate for one hour before rolling out to 1-cm thickness. Line a pie dish with pastry and cook in a medium oven, 180°C, until it hardens without browning.

While cooking the pastry combine all the filling ingredients. When the base is done, fill with the mixture and return to the oven at 190°C for 35 minutes.

Now mix the icing sugar with the grape liqueur. Allow tart to cook before icing. Decorate with walnut halves and liqueured grapes. Ambrosial!

Grapes in Gin

500 kg large firm grapes (not sultana)

1 cup white sugar

1 small orange (grated rind only)

enough gin to cover grapes

2 small sterilised clip-top jars

You'll be impressed with the full-bodied flavour of grapes liqueured in gin. And nothing could be easier!

Simply wash and dry a bunch of grapes for each jar, add the orange rind and sugar, cover with gin and clip the jars securely.

Allow to steep for at least one month. Carefully dissolve the sugar by gently stirring daily for the first couple of weeks.

If you are not giving the jars away as presents, try your hand at almond tuiles and/or pastry cream, see opposite and on page 48.

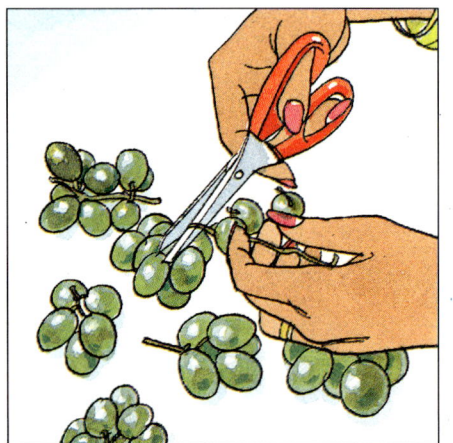

Opposite: *Almond Tuiles and Pastry Cream with Gin Grapes, page 48*

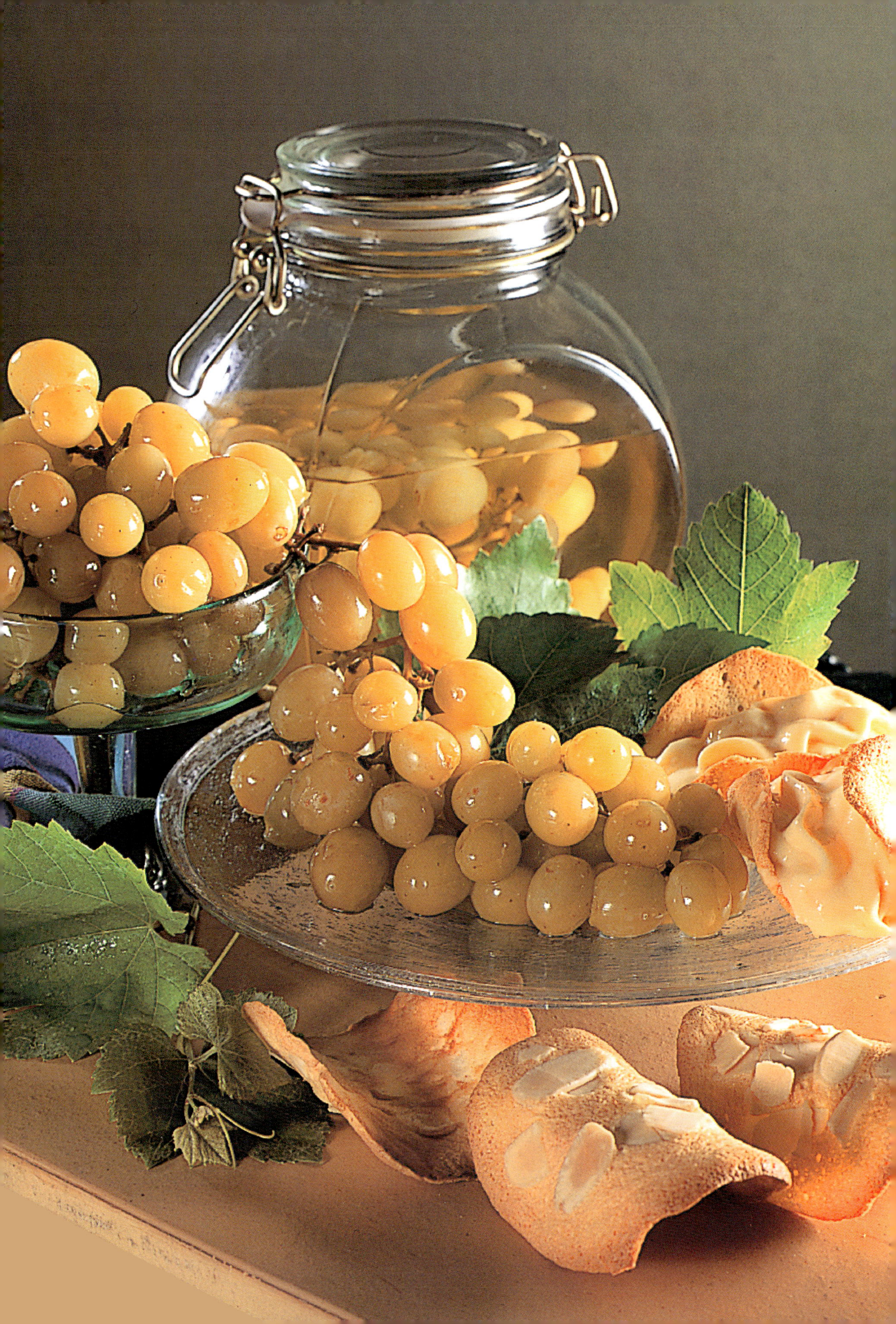

Almond Tuiles and Pastry Cream with Gin Grapes

Tuiles

95 g sugar
2 tablespoons flour
2 egg-whites
1¼ tablespoons melted butter
1 cup almond flakes

Mix sugar and flour and beat in egg-whites, one at a time. Beat well, add melted butter and stir in the flaked almonds.

Place generous teaspoonfuls of mixture on a greased tray. Cook only three at a time in a preheated 180°C oven for 12–15 minutes. Remove with a palette knife and, working quickly, place each biscuit around a glass jar or equivalent shape and form a tuile frill. Cool and store in airtight jar.

Pastry Cream

2 cups milk
½ cup sugar
8 pieces freshly-grated lemon rind
4 large yolks
½ cup flour
1 teaspoon vanilla essence
1 jar liqueured grapes

Put the milk, half the sugar and the lemon rind in a heavy-based saucepan and bring to boil. Remove from heat and discard rind.

In a bowl, whisk the yolks with the remaining sugar. Whisk in the flour, a tablespoon at a time, and continue whisking until the mixture is smooth. Whisk the hot milk, little by little, into yolk mixture and pour back into the saucepan.

Cook the cream/custard over a low to medium heat, stirring constantly until it thickens. Continue to cook over low heat for about 3 minutes. Stir frequently. Add vanilla.

Take off heat, stirring frequently until cool. This will stop a crust forming. Chill until ready to use. Can be made the day before.

Serve with a little pastry cream in each tuile and garnish alongside with liqueured grapes.

Grapes in Brandy

1 kg large green grapes (not sultana)

400 g caster or granulated sugar

enough brandy to cover grapes

1 large sterilised clip-top jar

Cut stems from large branches and wash and dry grapes. Roughly layer grapes and sugar in jar, stopping just short of the top. Cover with brandy, secure jar and allow to steep for at least one month.

I seldom use caster sugar with my liqueur fruit recipes, because it appears to set rather than float on the base of the jar. However, I sometimes use it with grapes and plums. Carefully dissolve the sugar by stirring daily for a couple of weeks.

Allow guests to pluck from a stem of grapes, or perhaps pluck and dip grapes into Roquefort fondue.

Brandied Grapes and Roquefort Fondue

50 g butter

300 ml white wine

25 ml brandy liqueur

400 g Roquefort or other blue cheese, broken into pieces

300 g Brie, rind removed and finely diced

pinch of salt

pinch of grated nutmeg

ground black pepper

1 medium jar liqueured grapes

Melt the butter in a fondue pot or heavy-based saucepan. Add the wine and brandy liqueur and bring to the boil. Reduce the heat and, in small amounts, whisk the cheeses until mixed smoothly together. Season with salt, nutmeg and pepper.

Spoon into small, individual soufflé dishes and place each on a sandwich-size plate. Garnish with a stem of liqueured grapes. A finger-food sensation!

Grapes in Grappa

500 g large firm grapes

1 cup sugar

1 small orange (grated rind only)

enough grappa to cover grapes

1 medium sterilised clip-top jar

Wash and dry little stems of grapes and loosely pack in jar, leaving a slight gap at the top. Sprinkle with orange peel and shake gently. Add sugar and cover with grappa. Secure well. Allow to steep for at least one month. Carefully dissolve the sugar by gently stirring daily for the first couple of weeks.

Enjoy your grapes and liqueur just like the Italian country folk do — simply sharing them with friends. On the other hand, serving them with chocolate truffles is a tempting option.

Chocolate Truffles with Liqueured Grapes

⅓ cup thickened cream

2 tablespoons liqueured grappa

200 g dark chocolate

4 tablespoons butter, softened

cocoa, powdered

1 medium jar liqueured grapes

Boil cream in a small, heavy saucepan until reduced to two tablespoons. Remove from heat. Stir in liqueured grappa and broken-up chocolate. Return to low heat and stir until chocolate melts. Whisk in softened butter. When mixture is smooth, pour into a shallow bowl and refrigerate until firm, about 40 minutes.

Scoop chocolate up with a teaspoon and shape into 5-cm length, egg-shaped balls. Gently roll in the cocoa. Place egg-shaped truffles in refrigerator. Stand at room temperature for 30 minutes before serving with liqueured grapes. It's worth the effort — you'll be richly rewarded for your trouble.

Grapes in Madeira

1 kg large firm grapes

2 cups brown sugar

2 cinnamon sticks

3 cloves

enough Madeira to cover fruit

1 large sterilised clip-top jar

The brown sugar makes a beautiful syrupy liqueur. Simply wash, dry and trim the grapes into small bunches. Loosely pack into jar, and add cinnamon sticks and cloves. Always leave a 2–3 cm space at the top of the jar. Pour sugar over and cover with Madeira. Clip jar securely.

Allow to steep for about six weeks. Carefully dissolve the sugar by gently stirring daily for the first couple of weeks.

After dinner, it's great to serve the liqueur with a grape floating on top. Used as a dessert, the grapes complete the flavoursome delight of hot cheese custard.

Liqueured Grapes with Hot Cheese Custard

4 yolks

300 ml milk

nutmeg

pepper

200 g gruyere cheese, cut into fine slices

1 medium jar liqueured grapes

Mix yolks with the milk. Add nutmeg and pepper. Butter an ovenproof dish and line with gruyere. Pour on egg mixture. Cover.

Bake in a 200°C oven for 20 minutes. Serve this reasonably thick custard with a few liqueured grapes and drizzle with liqueured Madeira. A warm-hearted dessert.

Grapes in Port

500 g large firm grapes

1 cup brown sugar

1 cinnamon stick

2 strips of orange rind

2 strips of lemon rind

enough port to cover fruit

1 medium sterilised clip-top jar

Wash and dry the grapes. Leave in small bunches, or have single grapes floating in the liqueur. Place grapes in jar with cinnamon sticks, lemon and orange peel, leaving a 2–3 cm space at the top of the jar. Pour sugar over and cover with port. Clip jar securely.

Leave for at least four weeks. Carefully dissolve the sugar by gently stirring daily for the first couple of weeks.

The deep-red port tends to lighten the colour of the grapes in the jar. Don't worry, the end result is a thick, wonderful liqueur with lusty and succulent grapes. These are delicious on their own, or blended with yoghurt.

Liqueured Grapes and Vanilla Yoghurt

1 kg container of vanilla yoghurt

300 ml whipped cream

2 tablespoons caster sugar

1 cup loose, drained liqueured grapes

4 teaspoons port liqueur

This is such an easy dessert that you hardly require a recipe. Simply mix the yoghurt, whipped cream and sugar together, and gently fold in liqueured grapes.

Place the mixture in four parfait glasses and top each with a teaspoon of your homemade port liqueur. Refreshingly simple.

Grapes in Sauterne

2 kg thick-skinned large white grapes

2 cups sugar

1 lemon (grated peel only)

enough Sauterne to cover fruit

2 large sterilised clip-top jars

Snip the grapes off the bunch, leaving a fraction of the stalk attached to each one. Be ruthless in discarding blemished or damaged grapes. They must be perfect or they will not liqueur well.

Rinse grapes in cold water, then dry thoroughly before carefully placing in jars without crushing. Add one cup sugar to each jar, remembering to stop fruit 2–3 cm from the top of the jar. Completely cover with Sauterne and clip jar securely.

During the next week or so, gently turn the jar upside-down once a day, and then return to the upright position. The sugar will eventually dissolve. Store for about three months. Simply served, they provide an excellent ending for a heavy meal. However, I prefer to make my other courses lighter so I can add them to an almond meringue.

Liqueured Grapes in Almond Meringue Slice

6 large egg-whites

pinch salt

375 g caster sugar

125 g slivered almonds

600 ml thickened cream

500 g liqueured grapes

1 teaspoon sugar

In a large bowl, beat the egg-whites with the salt until they stand in firm peaks. Fold in the sugar and almonds. Line two baking trays with baking paper and spread egg-white mixture evenly over them. Bake in a preheated slow oven, 140°C, for 75 minutes. Cool.

Beat the cream in a large bowl with a little sugar until it stands in peaks. Fold in the grapes. Place one of the meringues on a large, flat dish. Spread the cream and grape filling over it and top with the second meringue. Chill in the refrigerator until ready to serve. Cut into individual pieces and decorate each plate with a few liqueured grapes.

Muscatels in Brandy

400 g muscatels

1 cup brown sugar

1 cinnamon stick

½ small orange (grated rind only)

enough brandy to cover muscatels

1 medium sterilised clip-top jar

Muscatels are rather delicious by themselves, but even better when steeped in brandy. The resultant liqueur is also worth trying.

In this easy recipe you simply place muscatels in the jar with the cinnamon stick, orange rind and sugar. Cover with brandy and clip securely, remembering to leave a little space at the top of jar.

Over the next couple of weeks, once a day, turn the jar upside-down and then back to its upright position. This will help dissolve the sugar. Store for at least two weeks. Muscatels are delicious when served alongside whipped mascarpone sweetened with muscatel brandy liqueur.

Liqueured Muscatels on Mascarpone

250 g mascarpone cheese

3 tablespoons muscatel brandy liqueur

liqueured muscatel branches for garnish

Whip mascarpone and fold in liqueur. On individual cheese plates, place a spoonful of whipped mascarpone alongside a stalk of liqueured muscatels. Splendid simplicity.

Muscatels in Tokay

750 g muscatels

2 cups brown sugar

1 small lemon (grated rind only)

enough Tokay to cover muscatels

2 medium sterilised clip-top jars

My husband is keen on tawny port and Tokay. He often grumbles that somebody other than himself has been drinking his fortified wines. I just reply that the muscatels or prunes have. However, he doesn't complain when he's served a stalk of liqueured muscatels.

Halve the muscatels and place in jar. Add the lemon rind and sugar, and cover with Tokay. Leave a small gap between fruit and top of jars. Clip securely and store for at least two weeks.

Once a day over the next couple of weeks turn jars upside-down and back again. This will help dissolve the sugar. Serve with a warm Brie.

Warm Brie Filo with Liqueured Muscatels

12 sheets filo pastry

250 g butter, melted

1 Brie, whole (about 18 cm diameter)

1 medium jar liqueured muscatels

Preheat oven to 180°C. Butter a large baking tray.

Individually butter and layer six sheets of filo pastry. Place Brie in centre and fold edges of filo around it.

Butter remaining filo layers and place on top of Brie. Wrap around base of cheese. Bake for about 25 minutes, or until golden-brown. Stand for at least 15 minutes before serving.

Cut into individual wedges and drape liqueured muscatels on each slice. A wonderful, creamy fruit dessert.

Raisins in Muscat

375 g raisins

1 lemon (grated rind only)

3 pieces glacé ginger, finely chopped

enough muscat to cover raisins

3 small sterilised clip-top jars

Raisins are rather sweet, so I don't add sugar. But you can do so if you want to. Raisins also liqueur well, becoming quite potent, so don't eat many at a time. They are great to put in small jars and give away as presents. You can actually liqueur them one week and eat or give them away the following week!

Layer the raisins, lemon rind and finely-chopped ginger into the jar, stopping just short of the top. Cover with muscat and seal well. They will keep for at least a year. Liqueured raisins add a little potency to bread and butter pudding.

Bread and Butter Pudding with Liqueured Raisins

12 slices of bread, crusts removed

25 g unsalted butter

4 eggs

500 ml milk

125 g white sugar

125 g liqueured raisins, lightly drained

1 tablespoon brown sugar

1 tablespoon desiccated coconut (optional)

300 ml whipped cream

extra raisin muscat liqueur

Butter a pie dish. Lightly butter bread and cut into triangles. Line dish with one-third of the bread. With slotted spoon, ladle half of the raisins over the bread. Cover with another layer of bread and repeat the raisins. Finish with remaining bread.

Beat eggs, milk and sugar together and pour over pudding. Lightly sprinkle top with brown sugar and coconut. Place pudding in bain marie and bake at 180°C for 45–60 minutes.

Serve in pudding bowls and top with whipped cream that has raisin muscat liqueur folded through. A pudding to entice the taste-buds.

Grapefruit in Port

1 cup grapefruit

1 cup brown sugar

enough port to cover fruit

1 medium sterilised clip-top jar

When friends give me their homegrown grapefruit I usually liqueur some and eat the rest for breakfast. If I run short, I add orange flesh to the liqueur grapefruit.

Peel grapefruit including most of the pith. Place grapefruit on chopping board and turn and slice around outside. Don't chop too close to the centre, or you will end up with lots of pips. Discard centre.

Layer grapefruit and sugar, remembering to stop the fruit 2–3 cm from the top of the jar. Completely cover grapefruit with port and clip jar securely.

The sugar will quickly fall to the base of the jar. During the next week or so, gently turn the jar upside-down and back once a day to help dissolve the sugar. The fruit and liqueur will be ready in about three months.

Liqueured grapefruit is bitter-sweet and delectable when served with chantilly cream and coffee.

Port Grapefruit with Chantilly Cream

600 ml jar thickened cream

½ cup sour cream

½ cup caster sugar

2 teaspoons vanilla essence

grapefruit port liqueur

liqueured grapefruit

Combine thickened cream, sour cream, sugar and vanilla in medium bowl. Beat until soft peaks form. Refrigerate until ready to serve.

To serve: Place a scoop of cream on individual serving plates. Pour a little liqueured port around the cream. Decorate cream with liqueured grapefruit and citrus flowers or leaves. An excellent, tangy combination.

Grapefruit in Cointreau

500 g ripe, juicy grapefruit

2 cups brown sugar

3 cloves and 1 thin cinnamon stick

enough Cointreau to cover grapefruit

2 medium sterilised clip-top jars

Leave the grapefruit skin on — it acts as a firm, tasty garnish. Wash, dry and cut grapefruit into 6-mm slices. Layer these with the cloves and sugar. Place the cinnamon stick vertically through the layers.

Cover with Cointreau, leaving a 2–3 cm gap between grapefruit slices and top of jar. Secure the lid. Each day, for the next couple of weeks, gently stir the sugar on the base of the jar. This helps it dissolve.

Rich Cheesecake with Liqueured Grapefruit

Base

4 tablespoons butter

3 tablespoons sugar

1 egg, beaten

1 cup sifted flour

½ teaspoon baking powder

Cream butter and sugar until light. Add beaten egg, then sift together flour and baking powder. Add to the creamed mixture and stir until smooth. Pat firmly into a springform tin, covering sides and bottom.

Filling

250 g cream cheese

2 eggs, well-beaten

3 tablespoons sugar

2 tablespoons flour

2 cups milk

1 lemon, juice only

2 teaspoons grapefruit liqueur

1 medium jar liqueured grapefruit

Cream the cheese until soft. Add other ingredients, stir until smooth. Pour into unbaked pieshell and bake in a cool to moderate oven for about 90 minutes. Delicious served with liqueured grapefruit slices.

Grapefruit in White Curacao

2 cups grapefruit

2 cups white sugar

enough white Curacao to cover grapefruit

2 medium sterilised clip-top jars

Peel grapefruit including most of the pith. Place on chopping board and turn and slice around outside of fruit. Don't chop too close to the centre or you will end up with lots of pips. Discard centre.

Place a cup of grapefruit and sugar in each jar. Cover with white Curacao, leaving a small gap at the top. Clip jars securely. During the next week or so gently turn the jar upside-down and back, once a day. This helps to dissolve sugar.

Most liqueured fruit combines happily with cheese. Experiment with some of the more specialised varieites — goats' cheese, for example.

Liqueured Grapefruit with Creamed Goats' Cheese

125 g goats' cheese

4 tablespoons thickened cream

3 tablespoons caster sugar

segments of liqueured grapefruit

grapefruit liqueur

cinnamon for garnish

Blend cheese, cream and sugar into a smooth paste. Place mixture on individual serving plates, top with a couple of segments of liqueured grapefruit and drizzle a little liqueur over. Sprinkle with grated or ground cinnamon. A tangy and refreshing alternative.

Limes in Brandy

500 g limes

300 g brown sugar

2 cardamom pods

enough brandy to cover limes

1 medium sterilised clip-top jar

The fragrance of the cardamom spice gives the lime slices a lovely aroma as well as taste. Wash and dry limes and cut into 6-mm slices. Discard any pips or hard centres. Pack into jar, add cardamom pods and sugar. Cover with brandy, leaving a small gap at the top. Clip jar securely.

Because lime slices are rather delicate don't invert the jar. Just gently stir the sugar on the base of the jar each day for the next couple of weeks. Leave to steep for about six weeks.

A slice of liqueured lime is delicious when held by the skin and sucked. It also makes a wonderful garnish for chocolate mousse.

Chocolate Mousse with Liqueured Lime Slices

100 g cooking chocolate

2 tablespoons lime liqueur

1 tablespoon water

2 tablespoons caster sugar

1 egg-white

½ cup cream

1 medium jar liqueured limes

Melt chocolate with water and lime liqueur in a bowl over hot water. Add sugar, blend and cool.

Whip egg-white until stiff. Semi-whip cream. Whip cooled chocolate mixture, and gently fold in cream and then egg-white. Pour into four serving glasses and refrigerate until firm. Decorate with liqueured lime slices. A gratifying way to up your vitamin C.

Limes in Cointreau

1 kg limes

2 cups sugar

2 small dried lime leaves, or Kaffir lime leaves (available in Thai food shops)

enough Cointreau to cover limes

1 large sterilised clip-top jar

The lime leaves add a strong and refreshing flavour to this recipe. Wash and dry limes and cut into 6-mm slices. I leave the skin on, but if you prefer, remove the peel and then slice. Discard any pith or pips. Without over-packing the fruit, place limes in jar, add sugar and leaves and cover with Cointreau, stopping short of the top. Clip the jar securely.

To help dissolve the sugar on the base of the jar, gently stir with a spoon each day for the next couple of weeks. The longer you steep the limes, the stronger the flavour. Leave at least two months, if you have the willpower.

Liqueured Lime Custard Cake

1 whole egg

4 yolks

200 g unsalted butter, softened

250 g caster sugar

pinch salt

4 finely-chopped liqueured lime slices, rind included

350 g flour, sifted

300 ml milk, warmed

lime liqueur for drizzling

Beat whole egg and two yolks in a bowl. Add softened butter, 200 g of sugar, salt and chopped limes. Mix and then add 325 g of flour, until you have a smooth, shiny mix. Leave in a cool place for one hour.

Meantime, in a saucepan, beat the remaining sugar and flour with the other two egg yolks. Over a low heat, add the warmed milk. Keep stirring until you make a thick custard. Cool.

Grease a shallow cake tin and put in two-thirds of the cake mixture. Place custard on top and cover with the remaining mix. Bake at 200°C for about 40 minutes. Cool cake before taking from tin. Drizzle lime liqueur over individual slices.

Limes in Curacao

400 g limes

250 g sugar

2 cinnamon sticks

enough Curacao (Triple-sec) to cover limes

1 medium sterilised clip-top jar

Peel the limes and cut the flesh into chunks. Discard any pips or pith. Don't use the centre core, but squeeze over jar to use all the lime juice.

Place lime chunks in jar, add cinnamon sticks and sugar. Cover with Curacao, leaving a small gap at the top. Clip jar securely.

To help dissolve the sugar on the base of the jar, gently stir each day for the next couple of weeks. Store for at least six weeks.

Lime chunks are delectable when served with sweetened cream or, for a bit more sophistication, when used as a garnish on top of a chocolate cup filled with cream.

Chocolate Cups and Liqueured Lime Slices

150 g dark chocolate

15 g Copha (optional)

12 small foil cups

150 g cream, sweetened and whipped

12 chunks of liqueured limes

You will need an artist's paintbrush (fine) for this recipe. Place chopped chocolate and Copha in top of double saucepan and stir over simmering water until melted. Slightly cool.

Use brush to paint the chocolate on the inside of the foil cups, making sure the top edge is fairly thick. Leave in cool place to set. When firm use a skewer to peel away the foil cup. If the weather is hot, briefly put the cups into the freezer.

Fill chocolate cups with whipped cream and garnish with liqueured limes. Spoil your guests and serve the filled chocolate cups with coffee.

Oranges in Vodka

6 oranges

1½ cups sugar

1 cinnamon stick

1 teaspoon coriander seeds

enough vodka to cover oranges

1 large sterilised clip-top jar

As a substitute for vodka you could use white rum. The orange peel and coriander seeds give the orange chunks and liqueur a fresher, stronger flavour.

Without cutting into the pith, peel the oranges. Retain about one-quarter of the peel, cut into small strips and place in your jar. Now remove pith from oranges. Cut fruit into chunks and and discard any pips.

Add orange chunks, cinnamon stick and coriander seeds to jar. Pour sugar over and cover with vodka, remembering to leave a small gap at the top. Seal carefully and leave for two to three months.

Once a day, over the next few weeks, hold the jar on both the top and base and gently move the sugar around. It will eventually dissolve. Liqueured orange chunks add interest to a fresh fruit salad. Alternatively, place some on top of liqueured hazelnut cream.

Vodka Oranges on Liqueured Hazelnut Cream

1½ cups shelled hazelnuts (or hazelnut meal)

6 tablespoons corn syrup

3 tablespoons liqueured orange vodka

1 cup icing sugar, sifted

4 tablespoons butter, softened

liqueured orange chunks for garnish

To loosen skins, roast hazelnuts on a baking sheet at 180°C. This will take about 10–15 minutes. Take nuts from oven and cool slightly. Rub between towels to remove skins.

Grind hazelnuts in food processor until they form a paste. Place this in a bowl and stir in corn syrup and liqueured orange vodka. Stand for 20 minutes.

Cream icing sugar and butter until light and fluffy. Add hazelnut paste and mix throughly.

Simply place a scoop of hazelnut cream on individual serving plates and decorate with chunks of liqueured orange. Rich and satisfying.

Orange Slices in Cointreau

6 ripe juicy oranges
1 cup sugar
3 cloves
1 cinnamon stick
enough Cointreau to cover oranges
2 medium sterilised clip-top jars

Liqueured orange flesh is a wonderful colour additive to any dessert. Simply wash, dry and cut oranges into 6-mm slices. Layer slices in jar with sugar and cloves, stopping just short of the top. Place cinnamon stick vertically in centre. Cover with Cointreau and clip jars securely.

Once a day, over the next couple of weeks, gently stir the sugar on the base of the jar. It will eventually dissolve. Store for four to six weeks.

Orange slices can be used in a variety of ways — as decoration for cakes and desserts, or with chocolate or ice-cream.

Cointreau Orange Cake with Crème Fraiche

2 large oranges
250 g sugar
250 g ground almonds
1 teaspoon baking powder
6 eggs
1 jar orange Cointreau slices

Creme Fraiche

equal quantities of buttermilk and thickened cream (or buy a 300 ml carton of crème fraiche).

If you are making the *crème fraiche*, prepare the day before. Boil the oranges in water for about 90 minutes. Be sure not to boil them dry. Cool.

Preheat oven to 220°C. Drain and blend the oranges in a vitamiser or food processor. Add the remaining ingredients and mix thoroughly with the orange pulp. Pour into a greased 23-cm cake or springform tin and bake for one hour. Now combine equal quantities of buttermilk and thickened cream. Put in a cool place and stand for 1–2 hours. Refrigerate overnight before using.

Cool cake, spread top with *crème fraiche* and decorate with slices of orange liqueured Cointreau. An unbelievably moist orange sensation.

Oranges in Brandy

4 oranges, medium size

1½ cups brown sugar

1 teaspoon five-spice powder, or a few cloves and a cinnamon stick

enough brandy to cover oranges

1 medium sterilised clip-top jar

Wash and dry oranges and cut into 6-mm slices. Discard pips and tough centre. Layer orange slices, sugar and spice powder into jar, leaving a small space at the top. Cover with brandy and clip securely.

Gently stir with a spoon each day for the next couple of weeks. The sugar will eventually dissolve. Store for two months.

The orange slices are captivating on their own, and the liqueur is delicious. On the other hand, a slice on top of a moulded bavarois is also tempting.

Moulded Bavarois with Liqueured Oranges

250 ml milk

50 g caster sugar

3 yolks

6 g gelatine, dissolved in small amount of water

20 ml orange liqueur brandy

300 ml whipped cream

liqueured orange slices for garnish

In a saucepan mix caster sugar, yolks and half the milk. Bring the other half to the boil and stir into the saucepan mix. Add the dissolved gelatine and, on a low heat, cook gently until mixture coats a spoon. Do not bring to the boil.

Allow to cool. Stir from time to time to prevent skin from forming. When mixture begins to thicken, add orange liqueured brandy and fold in whipped cream. The custard and cream should form a homogeneous mix.

Spoon the bavarois into individual 200-ml lightly-oiled moulds (flat or funnelled). Cover and allow to set in refrigerator. When about to serve run a little warm water around moulds and shake bavarois free to break vacuum. Upend moulds on plates and garnish with one or two liqueured orange slices. A winner.

Oranges in Whisky

8 oranges, large but juicy

2 cups brown sugar

1 small lemon, (grated rind only)

2 cinnamon sticks

enough whisky to cover oranges

1 large sterilised clip-top or Mason jar

Remove orange peel, pith and pips. Use a sharp knife to cut oranges into segments between the membranes. Retain as much juice as possible. Layer fruit, any juice, lemon rind, cinnamon sticks and sugar, stopping just short of the top of the jar. Cover with whisky, seal and leave for three months. Once a day, over the next few weeks, hold jar securely on top and base and gently upend to dislodge the sugar. It will eventually dissolve. The liqueur makes a splendid after-dinner drink. Try the fruit with whisky cream, see opposite and on page 68.

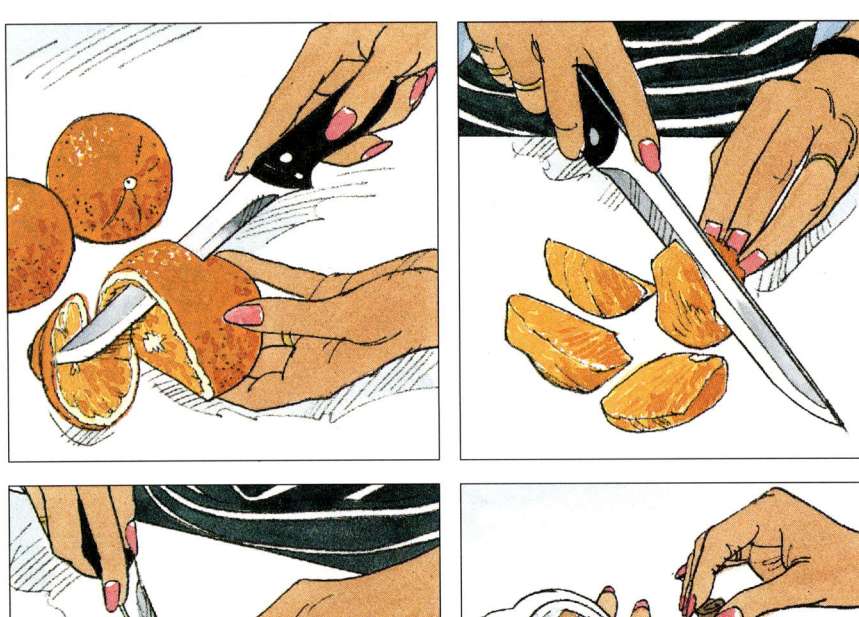

Opposite: *Liqueured Oranges in a Whisky Cream Mould, page 68*

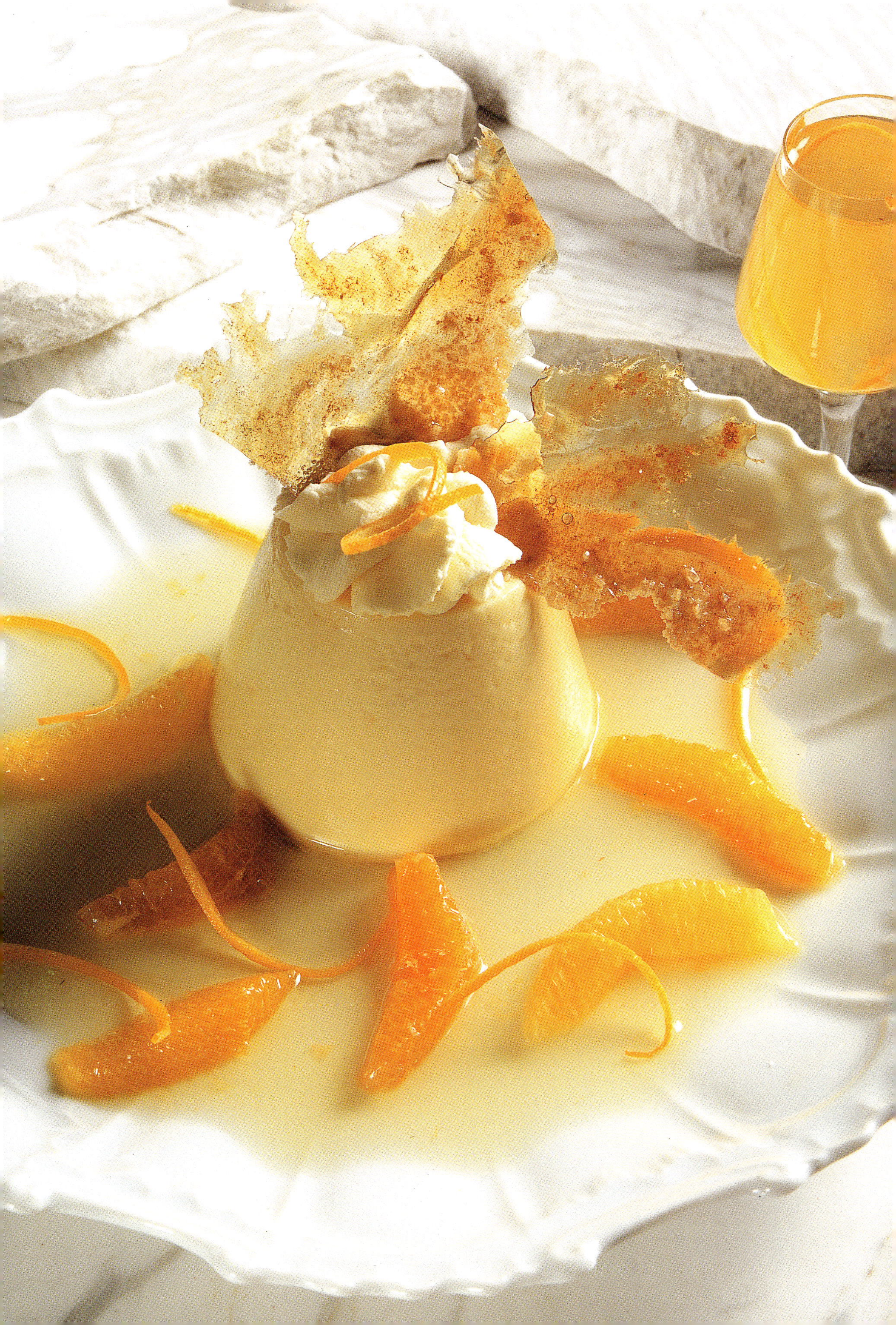

Liqueured Oranges in a Whisky Cream Mould

6 large yolks

3 tablespoons sugar

1½ teaspoons cornflour

400 ml thickened cream

75 ml liqueured orange whisky

3 tablespoons brown sugar

Sugar Bark

½ cup coffee sugar crystals

½ cup demerara sugar

½ cup caster sugar

300 ml whipped cream (optional)

liqueured orange segments, for garnish

Whisk together yolks, sugar and cornflour. In a small saucepan, heat the cream, but don't boil. Whisk it into egg mixture. Stir in liqueur, return the mixture to the saucepan and stir and simmer over a low heat until thick. Pour into six 200-ml moulds. Cool and refrigerate for 15–30 minutes.

Meanwhile, in a small bowl combine sugar bark ingredients. Sprinkle mixture evenly over lightly-greased foil. Place under hot grill until dissolved. (Watch constantly, otherwise sugar may burn.) Cool and break into pieces.

Upend moulds. Serve cold and decorate with sugar bark and cream if you desire. Pour a little liqueur around the base and garnish with liqueured orange segments. An easy dessert with exciting presentation and flavour.

Orange Fruit Mince in Brandy

3 oranges	225 g candied peel
1 lemon	225 g almonds, unskinned
450 g apples	100 g ground almonds
450 g currants	225 g brown sugar
450 g raisins	160 ml brandy
225 g sultanas	1 large Mason jar

Wash, peel, core and slice apples. Squeeze juice from lemons and oranges. Mix apples, currants, raisins and sultanas with fruit juices and put small amounts at a time into a food processor.

Chop the candied peel. Coarsely chop the whole almonds. Stir the peel, almonds, ground almonds, sugar and brandy into the apple mixture. Mix thoroughly.

Place mincemeat in Mason jar or smaller jars, leaving a small space at the top. Seal well. Store for at least one month.

Christmas Plain Cake with Orange Fruit Mince

500 g flour, sifted
25 g fresh yeast
150 g olive oil
125 g moist light brown sugar
1 teaspoon any fruit liqueur
some extra fruit liqueur for drizzling
1 large jar orange fruit mince

This is perfect for a special Christmas lunch with friends. Mix half the flour with the yeast and a little warm water. Cover with a cloth and leave in a warm place to rise overnight.

Mix the rest of the flour with the olive oil and sugar. Add the yeast mixture and fruit liqueur. Knead well, cover with a damp cloth and allow to double in size.

Divide the dough into six equal parts and shape each part into a ring. Link rings together to form a chain. Place on an oiled baking sheet and allow to rise for one hour. Then place in hot oven, 200°C, for 20 minutes or until a rich golden-brown.

Surround cake with orange mince. Serve each slice on its side, with extra liqueur drizzled over and a spoonful of orange fruit mince alongside.

Lemons in Cointreau

4 medium firm lemons

1 cup sugar

1 cinnamon stick, small

6 whole cloves

enough Cointreau to cover lemons

1 medium sterilised clip-top jar

Wash, dry and cut lemons into 6-mm wedges. Discard centre core and pips. Layer lemons, cloves and sugar in jar. Add small cinnamon stick and completely cover with Cointreau, leaving a 2–3 cm gap between unpeeled lemon slices and top of jar. Secure lid.

The sugar will quickly fall to the base of the jar. Don't be concerned. During the next week or so, gently turn the jar upside-down, and back, once a day. The sugar will eventually dissolve.

Lemons go well with crêpes, see opposite and on page 72.

Opposite: Crepini in Lemon-liqueured Juices, page 72

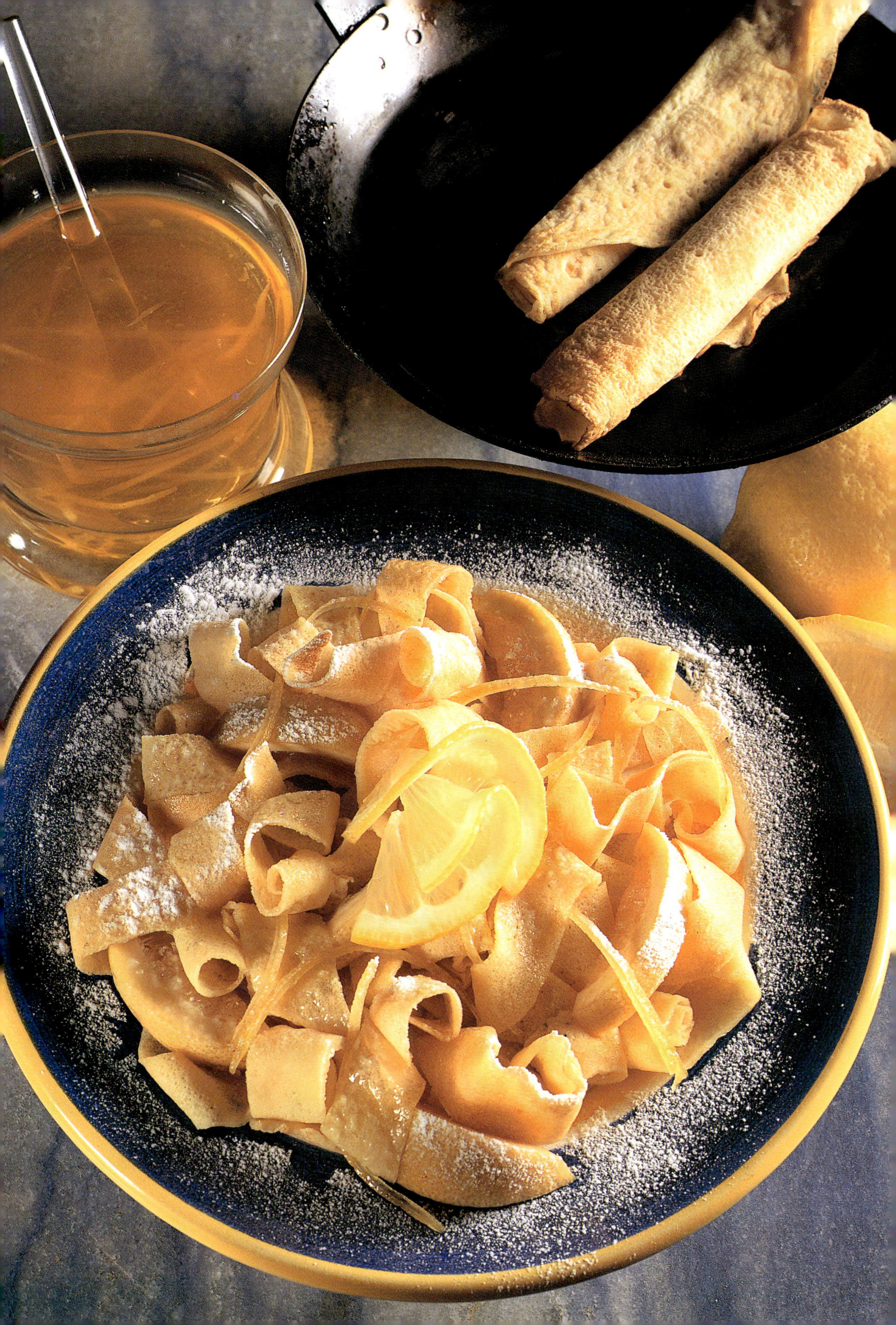

Crepini in Lemon-liqueured Juices

Crepini

40 g butter, plus extra for cooking

25 g flour

25 g cornflour

salt

250 ml milk

3 yolks

3 egg-whites

25 g sugar

Sauce

1 jar of liqueured lemons

icing sugar

I have called these pancakes *crepini* because they are so small. Melt the butter, sprinkle in the flour, cornflour and a pinch of salt. Stir thoroughly to make a smooth roux. Add the milk gradually, stirring constantly to ensure a lump-free mixture, and bring to the boil. Transfer the batter to a mixing bowl and beat in the yolks, one at a time.

Whisk the egg-whites until stiff, slowly adding the sugar, then gently fold in the whites, a little at a time.

Melt a small knob of butter in a frying pan and quickly fry two or three small *crepini* at a time, until golden on both sides. Keep them warm on a plate over a pan of simmering water.

Meanwhile, drain and gently warm the lemon liqueur. When warm, serve rolled *crepini* on separate plates, top with warm liqueur and decorate with liqueur lemon wedges. Sprinkle with icing sugar.

Alternatively, for a bit more flair, roll *crepini* and cut into 1-cm pieces along crêpe. Decoratively arrange on serving plates. Whichever way you serve the *crepini*, the lemon liqueur flavours are refreshing and delicious.

Prunes in Brandy

375 g prunes

1 cinnamon stick

4 cloves

½ orange, rind only

½ cup brown sugar

enough brandy to cover prunes

1 medium sterilised clip-top jar

With dark fruit, I prefer to use brown sugar — it makes a wonderfully thick liqueur. If stones are still in the prunes, gently remove them.

Layer prunes, sugar, cloves and orange peel in jar and place cinnamon stick about halfway. Fill the jar about three-quarters full and cover with brandy. Seal well and store for about two months. Every day, over the next few weeks, turn jar upside-down and back again. This will help dissolve the sugar.

Thick prune liqueur is a wonderful coffee accompaniment.

Pancakes with Liqueured Prunes and Ice-cream

250 g flour

2 eggs

1 tablespoon nut oil

1 pinch salt

1⅔ cup milk

butter for frying

vanilla ice-cream

1 medium jar liqueured prunes

It's important to rest a pancake mix, so make it early and leave for one hour before frying pancakes. Place flour in large bowl and make a well in the centre. Break in the eggs, add oil, salt and half the milk. Beat until smooth and then gently add remaining milk. Allow to stand for one hour.

While making the pancakes, place brandy prune liqueur and liqueured prunes in a heavy-based saucepan and gently warm through on low heat.

Butter a hot frying pan. Pour tablespoons of batter into pan and turn when bubbles appear. Serve with a little ice-cream on each pancake and pour over warmed brandy prunes and liqueur. Enticingly nutritious and delicious.

~ Prunes in Port ~

750 g dessert prunes
1 cup brown sugar
½ lemon (grated rind only)
2 pods vanilla (or cinnamon sticks if preferred)
enough port to cover prunes
2 medium sterilised clip-top jars

This recipe results in a very rich and velvety fruit liqueur. Prune stones may be left in or removed — it's up to you!

Divide between the two jars, prunes, sugar, vanilla pods and lemon rind. Leave a small gap at the top of the jars. Pour port over, seal well and leave for at least six to eight weeks. To dissolve the sugar, turn jars upside-down and back again, once a day, over the next few weeks.

Liqueured prunes are delicious with shortbread, cream or ice-cream, or with whipped mascarpone cheese, see opposite and on page 76.

Opposite: *Whipped Mascarpone with Liqueured Prunes, page 76*

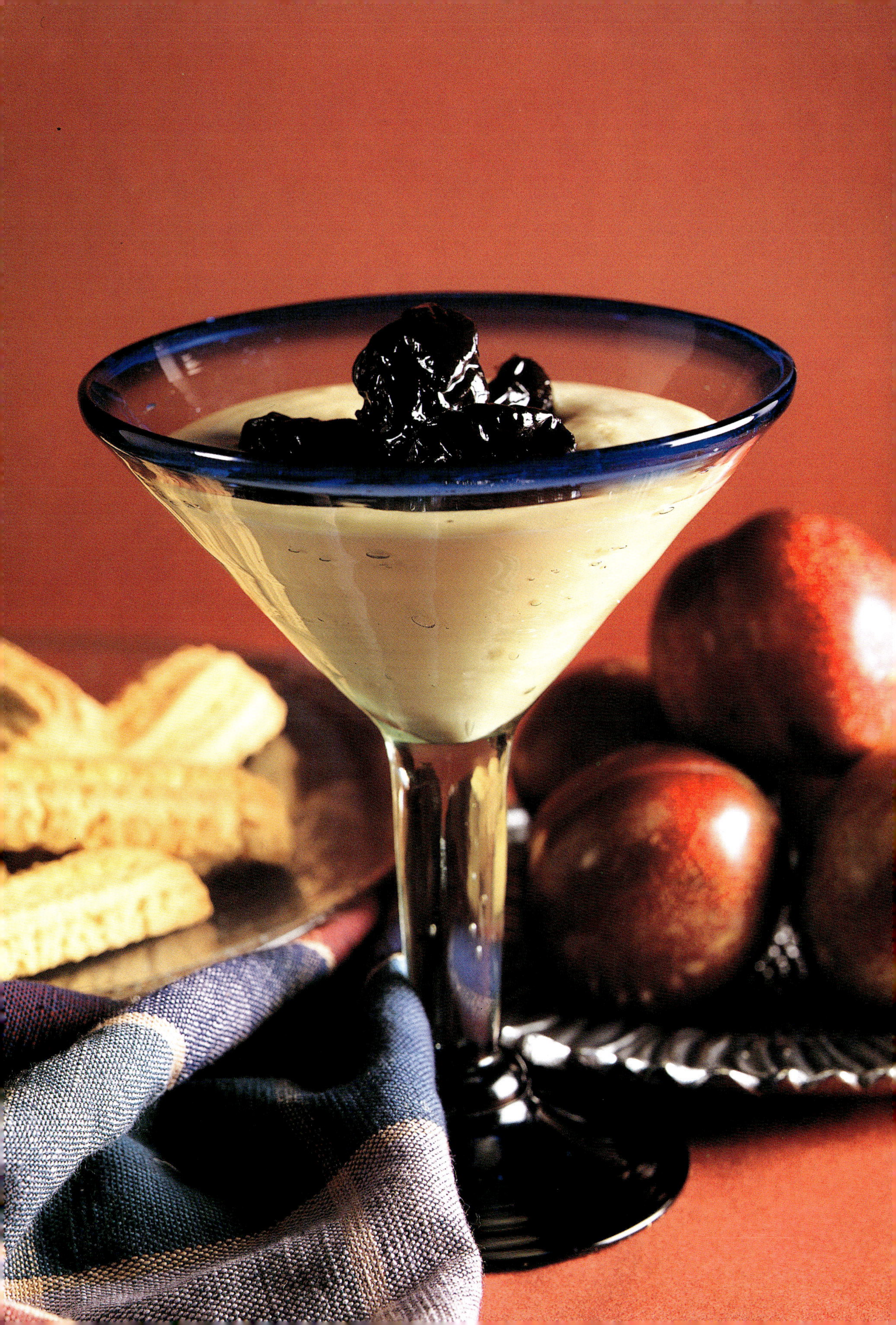

Whipped Mascarpone with Liqueured Prunes

5 yolks

1 cup sugar

750 g mascarpone cheese

1 medium jar liqueured prunes

Mascarpone is my favourite dessert cheese. It can simply be scooped from the tub and served with fruit, but I prefer its lighter consistency after being whipped. The pale ivory colour of this delightfully rich cheese perfectly complements port-liqueured prunes.

Beat yolks and sugar together until white. Add mascarpone bit by bit to mixture, and continue beating until it's smooth.

Place in individual bowls and refrigerate. Before serving, top with semi-drained, port-liqueured prunes. Simply superb!

Prunes in Marsala

375 g dessert prunes, stones removed

½ cup brown sugar

1 teaspoon Szechuan peppercorns

1 orange (grated rind only)

enough Marsala to cover prunes

1 medium sterilised clip-top jar

Layer prunes, sugar, peppercorns and orange rind in jar, leaving a small space at the top. Cover with Marsala, seal well and store for two to three months. Dissolve the sugar on base of jar over the next few weeks by daily turning jar upside-down and back again. Liqueured prunes look and taste so good that they can be used with most other dessert garnishes. Cream is great, but an orange cream adds that little touch of difference.

Orange Cream and Liqueured Prunes

2 dessertspoons gelatine, (use agar-agar if you prefer)

1 tablespoon water

4 yolks

1 cup caster sugar

1 cup orange juice

1 cup white wine

1 tablespoon lemon juice

300 ml thickened cream

1 medium jar liqueured prunes

Soften gelatine in water and leave. Beat yolks and sugar in top of double saucepan over simmering water until creamy. Remove from heat and pour in white wine. Return saucepan to the hot water and, stirring all the time, cook until mixture coats the spoon. Add gelatine and stir until dissolved. Add juices and stir well.

Pour into bowl and, when cool, chill in refrigerator until mixture thickens slightly. Whip cream, remove mixture from refrigerator and fold cream through. Return to bowl and chill until firm.

If you prefer warm fruit, place some Marsala prune liqueur and liqueured prunes in a heavy-based saucepan and gently heat through on low heat. When ready to eat, place a scoop of orange cream on individual plates and decorate with hot or cold prunes and Marsala prune liqueur. A sumptuous liqueured fruit affair.

Figs in Brandy

500 g dried figs

1½ cups brown sugar

enough brandy to cover figs

1 large sterilised clip-top jar

I have always used dried figs for liqueuring. Some people pour Kirsch over fresh figs — perhaps you'd like to experiment with that combination.

Place figs in jar and pour sugar over. Cover with brandy, leaving a small gap at top of jar. Clip jar securely.

Over the next couple of weeks, once a day, turn the jar upside-down and then back to its upright position. This will help dissolve the sugar.

After at least four weeks, serve figs with fresh cheese, or just nibble one when you feel like a small and tasty stimulant. I sometimes blend cream cheese with chopped pecans and serve with liqueured figs.

Liqueured Figs with Pecan Cream Cheese

250 g softened cream cheese

1 cup shelled pecans

1 medium jar liqueured figs

Chop pecans coarsely in a food processor. Add softened cream cheese and beat until smooth. Place in bowl, cover and refrigerate until ready to use. Serve with brandy-liqueured figs.

A heavenly self-indulgence!

Figs in Grappa

500 g dried figs

1½ cups white or brown sugar

½ cup ground walnuts and/or hazelnuts

enough grappa or vodka to cover figs

1 large sterilised clip-top jar

This is a traditional Turkish dessert. Cut out the figs' stalks. Fill each fig with some of the ground nuts. Layer in jar with sugar and cover with grappa or vodka. Don't completely fill the jar.

Over the next couple of weeks, once a day, turn the jar upside-down and then back to its upright position. This will help to dissolve the sugar.

Leave for at least a month before serving with fresh fruit or with gingered raspberry cream.

Liqueured Figs with Gingered Raspberry Cream

500 g liqueured figs

250 g raspberries

1 cup thickened cream

crystallised ginger for decoration

Arrange liqueured figs on individual plates. Purée and strain the raspberries. Discard the seeds. Whip cream and combine with puréed raspberries.

Spoon mixture around figs and decorate with finely-cut ginger strips. Wonderful, provocative flavours.

Figs in Madeira

1½ kg dried figs

750 g brown crystal sugar

300 g walnuts, shelled and halved (optional)

enough Madeira to cover figs

2 medium sterilised clip-top jars

I like to use brown sugar with figs because it makes a wonderful thick, dark liqueur. The walnuts are optional. You can either stuff them in each fig, layer them separately, or leave out altogether.

Cut the figs in half and push a half walnut into each. Press the two halves back together. Neatly layer figs with sugar, remembering to stop the fruit about 2–3 cm from the top of the jar. Completely cover fruit with Madeira and clip jar securely.

The sugar will quickly fall to the base of the jar. Don't be concerned. During the next week or so, gently turn the jar upside-down and back, once a day. The sugar will eventually dissolve.

The figs will be ready to serve with coffee or as cake decorations in three to four weeks. I sometimes put my Madeira figs into bliss balls. (Nearly any liqueur fruit can be added to this bliss ball recipe.)

Madeira Figs in Bliss Balls

500-g container of ricotta cheese

1 cup of chopped liqueured figs

1 cup desiccated coconut

3 tablespoons honey

Mix all the ingredients, except the coconut.

Form mixture into balls of 2.5 cm diameter and roll in coconut. Place in refrigerator. Serve bliss balls with a small glass of fig liqueur and/or coffee. Sensational and rather different.

Dried Fruit in Muscat

100 g dried apples

50 g dried pears

50 g dried prunes

50 g dried apricots

1 cup sugar

1 medium sterilised clip-top jar

1 cup muscat or enough to cover fruit

This easy recipe is ideal for times when fresh fruit is unavailable. You could liqueur the apples by themselves, but I prefer the combined flavours of the mixed fruit. Pricking dried fruit is not necessary.

Layer fruit and sugar in jar. Always finish fruit 2–3 cm short of the top of the jar. Cover with muscat and clip jar securely.

The sugar will quickly fall to the base of the jar. During the next week or so, gently turn the jar upside-down, once a day, and the sugar will eventually dissolve. The fruit will be ready to serve in four weeks.

Liqueured fruit salad is an easy appetising dessert. Included in a strudel, it's even more delectable.

Liqueured Fruit Strudel

1 packet ready-rolled puff pastry

1 yolk, beaten

1 medium jar drained liqueured dried fruit

icing sugar

300 ml cream

Pre-heat oven to 200°C.

Cut a 40-cm length of pastry. Place liqueured fruit on pastry sheet to within 4 cm of the long edges and 2 cm of the short sides.

Fold in short sides. Bring long sides together, and join by pinching top. Brush strudel with yolk. Place on greased oven tray.

Bake for 25–30 minutes or until the pastry is golden-brown. Remove from oven and cool. Sprinkle with icing sugar and serve with cream. Nourishingly splendid.

Pears in Grappa

1 kg firm pears

4 cups sugar

1 lemon, juice only

1 cup water

4 cloves

2 cinnamon sticks

enough grappa to cover pears

1 large sterilised Mason jar

I prefer to leave the pears whole in this recipe. Peel pears, but don't core them or remove stalks. Mix lemon juice and water together in large bowl. As you peel pears, put them in bowl. This prevents discolouring.

Place pears in jar with cloves and cinnamon sticks. Pour sugar over and cover with grappa. Leave a small space at top of jar, cover rim with plastic wrap and screw lid securely. Steep for at least two months.

Once a day, over the next couple of weeks, carefully hold top and base of jar and gently move the sugar from base. It will eventually dissolve.

Served at the end of a meal, a whole liqueured pear is a perfectly elegant and tasty dessert. For an extra touch of extravagance, serve them with an almond camembert.

Liqueured Pears with Almond Camembert

1 kg camembert (can be smaller but no larger)

1 cup grappa liqueur

150 g butter

120 g flaked and toasted almonds

liqueured pears for garnish

Place camembert in bowl, cover with grappa liqueur and leave overnight. Next day drain liqueur and roughly chop rind and cheese. Place in bowl with softened butter and beat until mixture is smooth. Refrigerate for 5 minutes.

Form cheese mixture into the original camembert shape and roll top and sides into the toasted almond flakes. Refrigerate and remove 30 minutes before serving. Slice cheese into wedges and garnish with pears. Extremely enticing. You'll want more!

Pears and Pineapple in Brandy

500 g firm pears
½ pineapple
2 cups sugar
enough brandy to cover pears
1 large sterilised clip-top jar

Wash, peel and core pears and cut each into about eight wedges. Peel pineapple until flesh is clean. Cut into thick slices and then cut each slice into six to eight triangles.

Layer pears and pineapple in jar, add sugar and cover with brandy. Leave a 2-3 cm gap at top of jar and clip securely.

Once a day, over the next couple of weeks, carefully hold top and base of jar and gently move the sugar around. It will eventually dissolve. It's great to combine liqueur fruits. These two, in particular, are fabulously punchy together. Simply delicious served on their own, or covered in a chocolate glaze.

Chocolate Glazed Liqueured Fruits

375 g chocolate (semi-sweet)
5 tablespoons Copha/vegetable shortening
4 slices pear/pineapple liqueured fruit for each serve
300 ml thickened cream, sweetened and whipped
extra chopped liqueured pineapple

Cover a baking sheet with tinfoil and place pears (cavity upright) and pineapple well apart. Melt chocolate and shortening in a bowl of simmering water, gently whisking all the time to keep mixture smooth. Cool slightly and pour over fruit. Coat the fruit without being too heavy-handed. Try not to get too much chocolate in the pear cavities. Set for at least one hour.

Carefully slide fruit onto individual serving plates and decorate with cream and some of the extra chopped liqueured pineapple. A chocolate lover's potion.

Pineapple in Kirsch

2 pineapples

½ cup sugar

½ lemon (grated rind only)

enough kirsch to cover pineapple

1 large sterilised Mason jar

I usually remove the pineapple cores. However, it is not necessary. They might be a little harder to chew, but the porosity of the pineapple steeps the core well. Peel pineapples, making sure the flesh is free from bruising. Cut 1-cm slices, and cut these into 1-cm × 2.5-cm lengths (approximately). Discard core.

Layer pineapple, sugar and lemon juice in jar. Cover with kirsch. Always remember to leave a 2–3 cm gap at the top of the jar. Clip jar securely and store at least four weeks. Because it's such a large, heavy jar it's probably best to use a large spoon to stir the sugar once a day for the next few weeks. Alternatively, tip gently and the sugar will eventually dissolve.

Biting into liqueured chunks is an exhilarating experience for pineapple devotees. The pieces also make a wonderful addition to frozen liqueured puddings.

Frozen Liqueured Puddings with Pineapple Chunks

1 egg

2 yolks

1 tablespoon pineapple kirsch liqueur

¼ cup caster sugar

6 chunks liqueured pineapple, finely chopped

200 ml vanilla or natural yoghurt

Most of my friends prefer vanilla yoghurt but you could try other flavours. Place whole egg, yolks, pineapple kirsch liqueur and sugar in warm bowl. Beat mixture until fluffy.

Blend pineapple and yoghurt well and add to fluffy mixture. Spoon into six crème caramel-sized moulds that can be placed in the freezer. Freeze for at least 2 hours.

When serving, quickly warm base of mould and upend onto individual plates. Decorate with chunks of kirsch-liqueured pineapple. A mind-blowing combination.

Pineapple in Brandy

1 pineapple

1 cup brown sugar

3 cloves

1 cinnamon stick

enough brandy to cover fruit

1 large sterilised clip-top or larger Mason jar

Peel pineapple, remove any bruising or 'eyes'. Cut into 1-cm slices. Layer pineapple, sugar, cloves and cinnamon stick in jar, leaving a small gap at the top. Cover with brandy and clip jar securely. Holding base and top of jar, roll sugar around once a day over the next couple of weeks to help dissolve the sugar.

Liqueured pineapple slices make an attractive snack.

Liqueured Pineapple Upside-down Cake

6 tablespoons butter

1 cup caster sugar

2 eggs

2 cups SR flour

¼ cup pineapple kirsch liqueur

¼ cup milk

Topping

3 tablespoons butter

½ cup brown sugar

450 g liqueured pineapple

This old-time favourite is easy and presents well. Beat butter and sugar to a cream. Add eggs, one at a time, and beat until light and fluffy. Sift flour. Combine syrup and milk. Fold into flour, and mix until smooth.

To make topping, cream butter and brown sugar. Spread over base of greased 20-cm cake tin lined with greased paper.

Drain the liqueured pineapple slices and arrange over brown sugar mixture. Carefully spread cake mixture over.

Bake in a moderate oven for one hour. Allow to stand 5 minutes before turning out on plate. Slice and serve with clotted cream. A very tasty splurge.

Berry Fruit in Framboise

250 g raspberries

125 g blueberries

125 g red currants

2 cups sugar

enough framboise (or maraschino) to cover fruit

2 medium clip-top jars

Don't wash fruit. Dry-wipe if necessary. The berries should have been picked so that stalks are trimmed to within a fraction of the fruit. The green calyx should also be carefully removed. Try not to crush the berries as you arrange them in separate layers. Cover each layer with plenty of sugar and finish 2–3 cm short of the top of the jars.

Cover fruit with liqueur and clip jars securely. For the next couple of weeks, gently tip the jars to the side and back from time to time. Leave to steep for two months in a dark, cool place.

Framboise is made from the essence of 20 kg of raspberries per bottle, so it really explodes with the smell and flavour of raspberries. Tempting when simply served with coffee or ice-cream. However, I prefer the full flavours when used in a summer pudding.

Summer Liqueur Pudding

450 g fresh raspberries and/or strawberries

50 g caster sugar

350 g drained liqueured berries

7–8 medium slices of white bread, crusts removed

4 tablespoons of berry liqueur

300 ml thickened cream

Lightly butter a 850-ml pudding basin. Place the fresh berries and caster sugar in a saucepan over medium heat and cook for 3–5 minutes. Remove fruit from heat and drain. Line pudding basin with bread, overlapping the slices and sealing well by pressing the edges together. Make sure there are no gaps in the bread. Place lightly-drained fresh and liqueured berries on bread, and add two tablepoons of berry liqueur. Then cover pudding with bread slices.

Place a plate on top (one that actually fits the rim of the bowl) and put a 1-kg weight on the plate. Refrigerate overnight.

To serve: Turn pudding out onto serving dish and spoon over the remaining two tablepoons of fruit liqueur. Cut into wedges and serve with thickened cream. A delightful, full-flavoured dessert.

Blueberries in Maraschino

500 g blueberries

500 g sugar

juice of ½ lemon and a few pieces of lemon peel

enough maraschino liqueur to cover fruit

2 medium sterilised clip-top jars

Wipe the fruit, but don't wash. Place in jars, alternating berries with layers of sugar, lemon juice and peel. Always finish fruit 2–3 cm short of the top of the jar. Secure lids and stand for 24 hours. Next day, cover berries with maraschino. Reseal jars and, for the following week, leave them in the sun or on a sunny windowsill for at least 2 hours per day. Over the next couple of weeks, tip jars to the side and back once a day to blend the sugar with liqueur.

The liqueur becomes fairly thick and the blueberries exude an exquisite aroma and flavour. The berries can simply be added to a fresh fruit salad, along with a little of the thick liqueur. Alternatively, a glazed blueberry liqueur tart is rather scrumptious.

Glazed Blueberry Liqueur Tart

Base

½ cup fine breadcrumbs

1½ cups SR flour

50 g sugar

½ lemon (grated rind only)

75 g butter

1 egg, beaten

1 medium jar liqueured blueberries

1 packet transparent cake glaze

Grease 36-cm flan tin or pizza tray and sprinkle with breadcrumbs. Mix flour, sugar and lemon rind. Rub in butter and and beaten egg. Mix well.

Firmly press onto tray and prick with fork. Cook 12 minutes at 180°C. Cool.

Drain blueberries well and place on cooked crust. Make up glaze according to directions, using liqueur instead of water and cover fruit. Decorate with cream. Subtle and superb.

Strawberries in Gin

4 cups strawberries

2½ cups sugar

juice of 1 small lemon

enough gin to cover strawberries

1 large sterilised clip-top jar

Lemon juice rather than lemon rind is added to this recipe because it's the basis for a strawberry granita. Eliminate the lemon if you don't want to make the granita.

Wash, dry and hull the strawberries. Place in jar and pour sugar and lemon juice over, leaving a 2–3 cm gap at the top. Cover with gin and seal carefully. To help dissolve the sugar, once a day for a couple of weeks, gently turn the jar on its side and back a few times. Steep for at least four weeks.

Liqueured strawberries make a most seductive finger-food. They also make a wonderful granita, which you can drink, or serve like a sorbet.

Gin-liqueured Strawberry Granita

½ large jar gin-liqueured strawberries

1 packet chocolate or wafer biscuits (optional)

Purée the liqueured strawberries. Freeze. (Granitas are just like a sorbet, except that they're ready straight after the second puréeing.)

When ready to drink or serve, take from freezer and purée again. Pack into chilled glasses. Drink straight away or, if used as a dessert sorbet, garnish with a chocolate or wafer biscuit. A great summer's day treat.

Strawberries in Sherry

500 g strawberries
1 cup sugar
enough sherry to cover strawberries
2 medium sterilised clip-top jars

On the whole, I don't like to use sherry for liqueured fruit. However, strawberries in sherry are an exception — they're delicious. But you could use kirsch or Madeira instead.

Hull, rinse and dry strawberries. Divide them in jars and sprinkle with sugar as you fill, stopping 2–3 cm short of the top. Cover with sherry and seal tightly.

To help dissolve the sugar, once a day for a couple of weeks, gently tip jars to the side and back a few times. Store for about five to six weeks.

It's hard to know which is best — the strawberries in sherry or the strawberry sherry liqueur. A sherry strawberry whip is not too bad either!

Sherry Strawberry Whip

2 medium jars liqueured strawberries
100 g natural or vanilla yoghurt
2 tablespoons skim milk
1 teaspoon gelatine or agar-agar
2 teaspoons water
1 egg-white

Blend one medium jar of drained, liqueured strawberries, skim milk and yoghurt in blender until smooth.

Sprinkle gelatine over water. When softened, dissolve over hot water. Cool. Add to strawberry mixture and mix well.

Softly beat egg-white and fold into strawberry mixture.

Lightly drain the second jar of liqueured strawberries and place a spoonful in the base of glasses or serving bowls. Top these strawberries with the strawberry mixture. Garnish with extra liqueured fruit or a mint leaf. Eat straight away or chill until ready. A tantalising treat for strawberry lovers.

Raspberries in White Rum

500 g raspberries

2 cups vanilla sugar

enough white rum to cover raspberries

2 medium sterilised clip-top jars

Berry fruits are so easy to liqueur. You can mix them together or keep them separate and, for a change, use kirsch or brandy instead of white rum. Vanilla sugar is caster sugar that's had a vanilla bean sitting in it. If you don't have any, use ordinary granulated sugar.

Wash, drain and hull raspberries. Layer raspberries and sugar and cover with white rum, leaving a small gap at the top of the jar. Seal tightly. Once a day for a couple of weeks, gently tip the jars to the side and back to help dissolve sugar. Store for at least four weeks.

Raspberries used in a champagne sabayon add a certain elegance to the end of a meal.

Liqueured Raspberries with Champagne Sabayon

1 medium jar of rum-liqueured raspberries

4 yolks

4 tablespoons sugar

5 ml brut (not sweet) champagne

Divide a jar of semi-drained raspberries in small heart-shapes or heaps on individual plates. Chill.

To make sabayon, combine yolks, sugar and champagne and place bowl over a saucepan of boiling water. Whisk vigorously until mixture is thick and fluffy. Pour around chilled raspberries. Lusty and colourful.

Blackcurrants in Aquavit

½ kg barely ripe blackcurrants

200 g sugar

enough aquavit to cover fruit

1 medium sterilised clip-top jar

Rinse blackcurrants in cold water and spread on paper towel to dry.

Layer fruit and sugar to 2–3 cm short of the top of the jar, being careful not to split skins. Cover with aquavit, and then clip jar securely.

To help dissolve the sugar, once a day for a couple of weeks, gently turn the jar on its side and back. Store in cool, semi-dark place.

Allow the fruit to steep for at least two months. I use blackcurrants for garnishing or in a fresh-tasting brûlé dessert.

Liqueured Blackcurrant Brûlé

1 jar of blackcurrants in aquavit

250 ml chilled thickened cream

125 g light brown sugar

Spoon semi-drained liqueured fruit into a lightly-buttered, one-litre gratin dish.

In a chilled bowl, beat cream until it holds peaks. Spread cream over fruit and chill in refrigerator for at least one hour.

Sift brown sugar over the cream and place under a preheated grill, about 10 cm from the heat. Brown about 2 minutes or until the sugar has melted. Serve on plain plates and garnish each serve with a red geranium flower. Simple and tastes great.

Blackcurrants in Grappa

2 cups firm blackcurrants

2 cups white or brown granulated sugar

enough grappa to cover blackcurrants

1 large sterilised clip-top jar

Because grappa is rather potent and dry I like to make the blackcurrants extra sweet in this recipe.

Wash blackcurrants and place on paper towel to dry, taking care not to split skins. Then simply place them in jar, leaving 2–3 cm at top. Pour sugar over fruit, cover with grappa, and seal tightly.

To dissolve sugar, gently turn the jar on its side and back once a day, for a couple of weeks. The sugar will eventually dissolve. Allow fruit to steep for at least two months.

Blackcurrants are great for a small, sweet nibble or placed on top of brandy baskets filled with cream.

Brandy Snap Baskets with Liqueured Blackcurrants

60 g butter

90 g caster sugar

1 teaspoon ground ginger

125 g golden syrup

60 g flour

1 medium jar liqueured blackcurrants

In a medium saucepan, combine butter, caster sugar, ground ginger and golden syrup. Heat gently until butter melts. Cool and stir in plain flour. Drop a heaped teaspoonful of mixture onto a baking sheet lined with baking paper.

Bake in a preheated, 180°C oven for 12 minutes or until the biscuit begins to darken around the edge. Cool a few seconds, then turn paper upside-down and peel away from the biscuit. The baking paper can be used again.

Working quickly before the biscuit sets, pick it up and mould over an upturned cup or mould, fluting out the edge. If the biscuit hardens before the cup is formed, return to the oven to soften. Just before serving, fill with cream and decorate with blackcurrants. An old favourite with a bit of spirit in the basket.

What to Do with Leftover Fruit Liqueurs

When you've eaten all your liqueur fruit you will sometimes have fruit liqueur left over in the jar. You can simply drink this as an after-dinner liqueur or use it as an ingredient in an aperitif. Alternatively, you can reduce and thicken it to make a wonderful sauce — ideal for pouring over ice-cream and other desserts.

How to Make Fruit Liqueur Sauces

Place a heavy-based saucepan on a low heat and pour in the liqueur. The longer you let the liqueur reduce, the thicker the sauce. A large saucepanful could take up to an hour. A small amount to pour over ice-cream could be less than 15 minutes.

The main reason for reducing the liquid is to have a thicker and clearer sauce. By that I mean, strained and without any fruit pieces. If you are reducing a reasonable amount of fruit liqueur, white scum (similar to that which forms on jam) will form. Gently remove it with a slotted spoon. When appropriate sauce consistency is reached, cool and strain into a sterilised bottle. The reduced liqueur will keep for at least twelve months, that is, if your friends don't raid your cellar!

Index

Alcohol, 8
Almond,
   camembert with liqueured pears, 82
   meringue slice and liqueured grapes, 53
   tuiles and pastry cream with gin grapes, *47*, 48
Amaretti biscuits with cumquats and cream, *11*, 12
Apricots,
   in brandy, 17
   in grappa, 14
   in Marsala, 18
   in vodka, 19
Armagnac grapes and walnut tart, 45

Bavarois with liqueured oranges, 65
Berry fruit in framboise, 86
Blackcurrants,
   in aquavit, 91
   in grappa, 92
Bliss balls with Madeira figs, 80
Blueberries in maraschino, 87
Bombe Alaska, 29
Brandied,
   grapes and Roquefort fondue, 49
   nectarines and profiteroles, 26
Brandy snap baskets with liqueured blackcurrants, 92
Bread and butter pudding with liqueured raisins, 56
Brie filo with muscatels, 55

Cheese custard with liqueured grapes, 51
Cheesecake with liqueured grapefruit, 58
Cherries,
   in brandy, 28
   in Grand Marnier, 29
   in grappa, 30
   in kirsch, 31
   in rum, 32
   in vodka, 33
Cherry,
   cake, 33
   chocolate cake, 32
   fruit mince in rum, 34
   liqueur money biscuits, 28
   mince with Christmas brandy sauce, 35, 36

Chestnuts,
   in Grand Marnier, 38
   in grappa, 37
Choc-a-holics' cherry chocolate cake, 32
Chocolate,
   cups and liqueured lime slices, 62
   glazed liqueured fruits, 83
   mousse with liqueured lime slices, 60
   truffles with liqueured grapes, 50
Christmas,
   brandy sauce with cherry mince, 35, 36
   plain cake with orange fruit mince, 69
Cointreau orange cake with *crème fraiche*, 64
Crème anglaise with liqueured chestnuts, 37
Crepini in lemon-liqueured juices, *71*, 72
Cumquats in brandy, 10
Custard,
   cake with liqueured limes, 61
   tart with vodka apricot, 19

Dried fruit, 9
   in Madeira, 20
   in muscat, 81

Figs,
   in brandy, 78
   in grappa, 79
   in Madeira, 80
Frozen,
   liqueured puddings with pineapple chunks, 84
   nut cream with liqueured peaches, 23
Fruit liqueur sauces, 93

Gelato, liqueured tangelo, 13
Gin grapes with almond tuiles and pastry cream, *47*, 48
Glazed blueberry liqueur tart, 87
Goats' cheese with liqueured grapefruit, 59
Grapefruit,
   in Cointreau, 58
   in port, 57
   in white Curacao, 59
Grapes,
   in Armagnac, 44
   in brandy, 49

in gin, 46
in grappa, 50
in Madeira, 51
in port, 52
in sauterne, 53

Hazelnut cream and vodka oranges, 63

Ice-cream,
  with liqueured cherries, 30
  with Madeira fruit, 20

Kirsch soufflé, 31

Leftover fruit liqueurs, 93
Lemons in Cointreau, 70
Limes,
  in brandy, 60
  in Cointreau, 61
  in Curacao, 62
Liqueured,
  apricot and sago pudding, *15*, 16
  apricots with mascarpone, 17
  blackcurrants in grappa, 92
  blackcurrants with brandy snap baskets, 92
  cherry bombe Alaska, 29
  cherry cake, 33
  cherry ice-cream, 30
  chestnuts on strawberry meringue torte, *39*, 40
  chestnuts with *crème anglaise*, 37
  cumquats with amaretti biscuits and cream, *11*, 12
  figs with gingered raspberry cream, 79
  figs with pecan cream cheese, 78
  fruit strudel, 81
  grapefruit with creamed goat's cheese, 59
  grapefruit with rich cheesecake, 58
  grapes and vanilla yoghurt, 52
  grapes in almond meringue slice, 53
  grapes with chocolate truffles, 50
  grapes with hot cheese custard, 51
  lime custard cake, 61
  lime slices and chocolate cups, 62
  lime slices with chocolate mousse, 60
  marshmallow cake, 25
  muscatels on mascarpone, 54
  oranges in a whisky cream mould, 67 68
  oranges with moulded bavarois, 65

peach sauce with snow eggs, 22
peaches in frozen nut cream, 23
peaches with meringue, 21
pears with almond camembert, 82
pineapple upside-down cake, 85
plum sorbet, 24
plums with marshmallow cake, 25
prunes and orange cream, 77
prunes with mascarpone, 75, 76
prunes with pancakes and ice-cream, 73
raisins with bread and butter pudding, 56
raspberries with champagne, 90
tangelo gelato, 13

Madeira,
  figs in bliss balls, 80
  fruit ice-cream, 20
Marsala apricots and zabaglione, 18
Marshmallow cake with liqueured plums, 25
Mascarpone,
  with liqueured apricots, 17
  with liqueured muscatels, 54
  with liqueured prunes, 75, 76
Money biscuits, 28
Morello cherries in rum, 32
Mousse with brandied nectarines, 27
Muscatels,
  in brandy, 54
  in Tokay, 55

Nectarine brandy mousse, 27
Nectarines,
  in brandy, 26
  in peach brandy, 26

Orange,
  cake, 64
  cream and liqueured prunes, 77
  fruit mince in brandy, 69
  slices in Cointreau, 64
Oranges,
  in brandy, 65
  in vodka, 63
  in whisky, 66

Pancakes with liqueured prunes and ice-cream, 73
Passionfruit in white rum, 42
Peaches,

in brandy, 21
in Grand Marnier, 22
in Marsala, 23
Pears,
    and pineapple in brandy, 83
    in grappa, 82
Pecan cream cheese with liqueured figs, 78
Pineapple,
    and pears in brandy, 83
    chunks with frozen liqueured puddings, 84
    in brandy, 85
    in kirsch, 84
Plums,
    in aquavit, 24
    in brandy, 25
Port grapefruit with chantilly cream, 57
Profiteroles filled with brandied nectarines, 26
Prunes,
    in brandy, 73
    in Marsala, 77
    in port, 74

Quinces,
    in jelly russe with sponge fingers, 41
    in vodka, 41

Raisins in muscat, 56
Raspberries in white rum, 90
Rich cheesecake with liqueured grapefruit, 58
Roquefort fondue with brandied grapes, 49

Sabayon, 90
Sago and liqueured apricot pudding, 15, 16
Sherry strawberry whip, 89
Snow eggs with liqueured peach sauce, 22
Sorbet, liqueured plum, 24
Soufflé,
    passionfruit, 43, 44
    with liqueured cherries, 31
St Valentine's Day passion soufflé, 43, 44
Sterilising jars, 8
Strawberries,
    in gin, 88
    in sherry, 89
Strawberry,
    granita, 88

meringue torte with liqueured chestnuts, 39, 40
Strudel, 81
Sugar bark, 68
Summer liqueur pudding, 86

Tangelo gelato, 13
Tangelos in white curacao, 13

Upside-down cake, 85

Vodka,
    apricot custard tart, 19
    oranges on liqueured hazelnut cream, 63

Walnut tart and Armagnac grapes, 45
Warm Brie filo with liqueured muscatels, 55
Warmed liqueured peaches with meringue, 21
Whipped mascarpone with liqueured prunes, 75, 76
Whisky cream mould with liqueured oranges, 67, 68

Yoghurt and liqueured grapes, 52

Zabaglione and Marsala apricots, 18